SOLIMAN AND PERSEDA
[1592/93]

THE MALONE SOCIETY
REPRINTS, VOL. 181
2014

PUBLISHED FOR THE MALONE SOCIETY
BY MANCHESTER UNIVERSITY PRESS

Oxford Road, Manchester M13 9NR, UK
and Room 400, 175 Fifth Avenue, New York, NY 10010, USA
www.manchesteruniversitypress.co.uk

Distributed exclusively in the USA by
Palgrave, 175 Fifth Avenue, New York,
NY 10010, USA

Distributed exclusively in Canada by
UBC Press, University of British Columbia, 2029 West Mall,
Vancouver, BC, Canada V6T 1Z2

British Library Cataloguing-in-Publication Data
A catalogue record for this book is available from the British Library

Library of Congress Cataloging-in-Publication Data applied for

ISBN 978-0-7190-9585-6

Typeset by New Leaf Design, Scarborough, North Yorkshire

Printed by Berforts Information Press Ltd, Oxford

This edition of *Soliman and Perseda* was prepared by Lukas Erne, and checked by G. R. Proudfoot and H. R. Woudhuysen. The Society is grateful to the British Library for permission to reproduce their copy of the play (C.34.b.44).

March 2014   G. R. PROUDFOOT

INTRODUCTION

Soliman and Perseda was entered in the Stationers' Register on 20 November 1592 to Edward White.[1] The entry reads: 'Edward White. Entred for his Copie vnder than*des* of the Bisshop of London and m^r warden Styrropp | the trage- dye of Salamon and Perceda'.[2] Two early editions survive, one undated and one dated 1599. Of the undated edition, only one copy is extant, now in the British Library (shelfmark, C.34.b.44), of which the present edition is a 1:1 facsimile. The copy was previously part of David Garrick's collection of old plays.[3] It has the following title-page:

[in a compartment] THE | TRAGEDYE OF | *SOLYMAN* AND | *PERSEDA*. | *VVherein is laide open, Loues* | constancy, Fortunes incon- | stancy, and Deaths | Triumphs. | [ornament] | AT LONDON | Printed by *Edward Allde* for | Edward White, and are to be solde at | the little North doore of Paules | Church, at the signe of | the Gun.

The head-title on A2^r reads: '[ornament] T H E | Tragedie of *Soliman* and | *Perseda*.' The text ends with the following colophon: '[ornament] Imprinted at London for *Edward* | White, and are to be sold at his shop, at the | little North doore of S.Paules Church | *at the signe of the Gunne*.' (I2^v). The edition collates A–H^4 I^2 (A–H signed $1–3) and has thirty-four unnumbered leaves.

The collation and the number of leaves of the 1599 edition are identical. It too was printed by Allde for White, and the title-page differs little from that of the undated edition:

[in a compartment] THE | TRAGEDIE | OF *SOLIMON* AND | *PERSEDA*. | *VVherein is laide open, Loues* | constancie, Fortunes incon- | stancie, and Deaths | Triumphs. | [ornament] | AT LONDON | Printed by *Edward Allde*, for | Edward White, and are to be solde at | the little North doore of Paules Church, | at the signe of the Gun.

The colophon mentions the date of publication: 1599. A second issue of this edi- tion adds a line of small type on the title-page, after 'Triumphs.': 'Newly corrected

---

[1] Modern scholars have variously called the play '*Soliman and Perseda*' or '*Solyman and Perseda*'. The name of the Turkish emperor is spelled '*SOLYMAN*' on the title-page of the undated edition, but the head-title on A2^r has '*Soliman*', and the running title—which is '*The Tragedie | of Soliman and Perseda*.' throughout—adopts the same spelling. In the rest of the play, including speech headings, the name is spelled sixteen times with 'y' but 148 times with 'i'. '*Soliman*' is thus the dominant spelling, which is why the title adopted here is '*Soliman and Perseda*'.

[2] W. W. Greg, *A Bibliography of the English Printed Drama to the Restoration*, 4 vols (London, 1939–59), I.8.

[3] See George M. Kahrl with Dorothy Anderson, *The Garrick Collection of Old English Plays: A Catalogue with an Historical Introduction* (London, 1982), p. 247.

and amended.' W. W. Greg noted that the line was 'stamped in, apparently by hand, after the sheet was printed'.[4]

After the second quarto, *Soliman and Perseda* was next reprinted in 1773, when it appeared in the second volume of Thomas Hawkins's edition of *The Origin of the English Drama* (pp. 195–284).[5] This edition, as Hawkins writes in his preface, is based on Garrick's copy of the 1599 quarto now in the British Library (shelfmark C.34.b.45). Hawkins was the first to add a 'DRAMATIS PERSONAE' list; he divided the play into five acts, modernized the spelling, and made a number of emendations. When W. Carew Hazlitt added *Soliman and Perseda* to *A Select Collection of Old English Plays* (1874), vol. 5, pp. 253–374, the fourth, revised and enlarged edition of Robert Dodsley's collection originally published in 1744, he reprinted Hawkins's preface and, like Hawkins, showed no awareness of any other early edition than that of 1599.[6] Hazlitt usually followed Hawkins's text but provided light annotation and a number of additional emendations.

Between Hawkins's edition of 1773 and his own death in 1809, Joseph Smeeton had published a type-facsimile reprint of the 1599 edition of *Soliman and Perseda*.[7] Although Smeeton had no intention of deceiving his readers, and some copies indeed bear an imprint reading 'J. Smeeton, Printer, St. Martin's Lane' on the verso of the title-leaf, two copies of the facsimile were miscatalogued in the British Museum as copies of the original. When F. S. Boas edited the play for *The Works of Thomas Kyd*, published by Oxford University Press in 1901, he mistook Smeeton's facsimile for an early edition and adopted a number of readings from it.[8] Confusion did not stop there:

[4] Greg, *Bibliography*, 1.187. Copies of the first issue are now among the holdings of the following institutions: Trinity College, Cambridge; Canterbury Cathedral; Chapin Library, Williams College, Williamstown, MA; National Library of Scotland, Edinburgh; Folger Shakespeare Library, Washington, DC; Harvard University, Cambridge, MA; Huntington Library, San Marino, CA; University of Illinois, Urbana, IL; British Library, London; Dyce Collection, Victoria and Albert Museum, London; Royal Holloway, University of London; Bodleian Library, Oxford; and Queen's College, Oxford. Copies of the second issue are at Boston Public Library, Boston, MA; Folger Shakespeare Library, Washington, DC; University of Illinois, Urbana, IL; Huntington Library, San Marino, CA; British Library, London; and Harry Ransom Center, University of Texas, Austin, TX.

[5] The only exception to this are nine one-line excerpts from the play that were included (some in adapted form) in the commonplace book *Bel-vedére, or The garden of the Muses* (STC 3189) of 1600: 'Vertue doth neuer enuie good desert.' (C2ʳ, cf. TLN 462); 'Loues workes are more than of a mortall temper.' (C8ᵛ, cf. TLN 703); 'Where any may liue well, that is his countrey.' (E8ᵛ, cf. TLN 1783); 'What boots complaining, where's no remedie?' (F5ᵛ, cf. TLN 2028); 'A hard attempt to tempt a foe for aid.' (G8ʳ, cf. TLN 1025); 'Young slippes are neuer graft in windie dayes' (K3ʳ, cf. TLN 136); 'Our inward cares are most pent in with griefe.' (K8ʳ, cf. TLN 825); 'The greatest losses seldome are restor'd' (L3ᵛ, cf. TLN 564); and 'The shrub is safe, when the tall Cedar shakes.' (N8ʳ, cf. TLN 2187).

[6] Hazlitt mistakenly held that 'there was only one impression, which received no fewer than three title-pages' (p. 254).

[7] Ronald B. McKerrow dated Smeeton's facsimile edition 'about 1815' (*An Introduction to Bibliography for Literary Students* (Oxford, 1927), p. 231) and Arthur Freeman 'About 1810' (*Thomas Kyd: Facts and Problems* (Oxford, 1967), p. 156); for the date of Smeeton's death, see *The Gentleman's Magazine*, vol. 79 (1809), pp. 474, 486.

[8] A. T. Hazen, 'Type-Facsimiles', *Modern Philology*, 44 (1947), 209–17, 210.

when John Stephen Farmer, in 1912, published an edition of *Soliman and Perseda*, 1599, in collotype as part of the 'Tudor Facsimile Texts' series, he inadvertently reproduced a copy of Smeeton's facsimile.[9]

Boas was the first to attempt a collation of all editions. He writes in the 'Editor's Note' that the 'text adopted' by him 'is that of the undated Quarto' and that he has 'reproduced the original spelling',[10] yet his text contains many errors.[11] John J. Murray's edition of the play, published in 1991 and based on a Ph.D. thesis of 1959, with more than sixty substantial verbal errors, is textually even less reliable than Boas's.[12] His 'Textual Notes' consist chiefly of accidental variants and exclude mention of Hawkins and Hazlitt, with the result that the many readings assigned to Boas include quite a few that did not originate with him. Nor does Murray record his own emendations in the 'Textual Notes'. Thus neither Boas nor Murray, any more than their eighteenth- and nineteenth-century predecessors, produced a reliable text based on the earliest quarto of *Soliman and Perseda*.[13]

In 1773, Thomas Hawkins was the first to argue for Thomas Kyd's authorship: 'might the editor be allowed to indulge a conjecture, he would ascribe

[9] John S. Farmer (ed.), *The Tragedye of Solyman and Perseda*, Tudor Facsimile Texts (Amersham, 1912). For the Smeeton type-facsimile and the editorial confusion to which it led, see W. W. Greg's review of Boas's *The Works of Thomas Kyd* in *Modern Language Quarterly*, 4 (1901), 185–90; McKerrow, *An Introduction to Bibliography*, pp. 231–2; Hazen, 'Type-Facsimiles'; and Freeman, *Thomas Kyd*, p. 156; Boas acknowledged his error in the 'Corrections and Additions' added to the 1955 reprint of *The Works of Thomas Kyd* (p. cxxv).

[10] Boas (ed.), *The Works of Thomas Kyd*, pp. 162, vii.

[11] See 'I not' (1.1.18) / 'not I' (TLN 39); 'heauen' (1.3.134) / 'heauens' (TLN 305); *the Prince of Cypris* (1.4.0.1) / *not in Q1* (TLN 422); 1.4.46 *no exit SD for Ferdinando* / *'Exit.'* (TLN 470); 1.4.70 *no SD* / *'Exit.'* (TLN 496); 'and' (1.4.81) / 'but' (TLN 510); 1.4.137 *no SD* / *'Exit.'* (TLN 571); *'Ferdinando'* (2.1.8) / *'Fernando'* (TLN 741); 'the' (2.1.23) / 'these' (TLN 756); 'me' (2.1.173) / 'to me' (TLN 914); 'Guelpio, Iulio' (2.1.200.1) / Guelpio *and* Iulio' (TLN 943); 'while' (2.1.307) / 'whilst' (TLN 1065); 'a disgrace' (2.2.89) / 'disgrace' (TLN 1194); 'be' (3.1.8) / 'he' (TLN 1226); 'each one' (3.3.21) / 'one' (TLN 1409); 'withould' (4.1.115) / 'withhould' (TLN 1622); 'Graunt <me>' (4.1.140; *the addition of* 'me' *is wrongly assigned to Hawkins*) / 'Graunt me' (TLN 1650); 'Reuiues' (4.1.191) / 'Reuies' (TLN 1703); 'But' (4.1.201) / 'And' (TLN 1713); *'Exeunt.'* (4.1.202) / *SD one line later* (TLN 1715); 'your loue' (4.1.238) / 'her loue' (TLN 1750); 'pin proofe' (4.2.39) / 'pin prooue' (TLN 1818); 'you not' (4.2.64) / 'not you' (TLN 1848); 'I will' (4.2.74) / 'ile' (TLN 1859); 'And' (5.1.10) / 'But' (TLN 1899); 'when' (5.2.21) / 'where' (TLN 1962); 'he' (5.2.42) / 'we' (TLN 1983); 'I will' (5.4.28) / 'ile' (TLN 2227); 'ouer match' (5.4.32) / 'ouermatch' (TLN 2231).

[12] John J. Murray (ed.), *The Tragedye of Solyman and Perseda* (New York, 1991). See, for instance, 'loue' (1.1.21) / 'long loue' (TLN 42); *no SD* (1.4.70) / *'Exit.'* (TLN 496); 'do not' (1.4.96) / 'do' (TLN 525); 'compassion' (1.6.8) / 'compression' (TLN 700); *no SD* (2.3.19) / *Exeunt.* (TLN 1217); 'my' (3.1.109) / 'thy' (TLN 1329); *a line missing after* 4.1.14 / 'Of honors titles, or of wealth, or gaine,' (TLN 1521); 'See' (5.2.5) / 'Come fellowes see' (TLN 1945); 'seruitour' (5.3.8) / 'true seruitour' (TLN 2104); *a line missing after* 5.3.49 / 'Theres a reward for all thy treasons past,' (TLN 2151); 'my' (5.3.79) / 'My fathers sonne, my' (TLN 2190); 'cannot runne' (5.3.80–1) / 'cannot speake, / And he can doe lesse that cannot runne' (TLN 2191–2); *SD missing before* 5.4.1 / *'Enter* Soliman, Brusor, with *Ianisaries.'* (TLN 2196); *a line missing after* 5.5.21 / 'VVheres *Basilisco* but in my triumph?' (TLN 2385).

[13] Arthur Freeman's planned new Oxford edition of Kyd's works, which promised a reliably based text of *Soliman and Perseda*, was unfortunately abandoned (see Arthur Freeman, 'The Printing of *The Spanish tragedy'*, *The Library*, 5th ser., 24 (1969), 187–99, p. 187 n. 4).

it to *Kyd*, as it carries with it many internal marks of that author's manner of composition'. Hawkins noted that 'in *The Spanish Tragedy* the story of *Erastus* and *Perseda* is introduced by *Hieronimo* in the play-within-the-play.[14] F. S. Boas endorsed Hawkins's argument, as did Murray.[15] Moreover, Arthur Freeman's scholarly monograph on Kyd analyses the play's many similarities with *The Spanish Tragedy*, the 'coincidence of plot', 'similarities in dramatic technique', 'characteristics of melodrama and dramatic irony', the 'superstructure of allegorical figures', 'coincidences in language, style, versification, and terminology' as well as the 'parallel use of comparatively uncommon rhetorical figures', and concludes that 'The weight of the evidence is definitely for Kyd's authorship of *Soliman*'.[16] In recent years, computer-assisted analysis by MacDonald Jackson, Thomas Merriam, Brian Vickers and Ward E. Y. Elliott, and Robert J. Valenza has corroborated the case for Kyd's authorship of *Soliman and Perseda*.[17]

As early as 1965, but unnoticed by Kyd scholars of the later twentieth century, Helen Gardner found a piece of external evidence linking *Soliman and Perseda* to Kyd. Gardner was building on Herbert J. C. Grierson's discovery that John Donne's elegy 'The Bracelet: Upon the Losse of his Mistresses Chaine, for Which he Made Satisfaction' mocks Erastus' loss and recovery of the bracelet he received from Perseda.[18] As Gardner points out, a passage in 'The Bracelet'—'libels, or some interdicted thing, | Which negligently kept, thy ruine bring' (ll. 101–2)—is likely to constitute 'a topical reference to the misfortunes that befell Kyd in 1593',[19] when Kyd had his chambers searched for a 'libell that concern'd the state', leading to his imprisonment, the loss of his patron and his death in the following year.[20] Gardner concludes that 'it is difficult not to see a reference in Donne's lines to Kyd's negligent

---

[14] Hawkins (ed.), *The Origin of the English Drama*, 2.197.

[15] Boas (ed.), pp. lx–lxi; Murray, pp. xxvi–xxxiii.

[16] Freeman, *Thomas Kyd*, pp. 140–2, 146.

[17] MacDonald P. Jackson, 'New Research on the Dramatic Canon of Thomas Kyd', *Research Opportunities in Renaissance Drama*, 47 (2008), 107–27; Thomas Merriam, 'Possible Light on a Kyd Canon', *Notes and Queries*, 240 [N.S. 42] (1995), 340–1; Brian Vickers, 'Thomas Kyd, Secret Sharer', *The Times Literary Supplement*, 18 April 2008, pp. 13–15; Ward E. Y. Elliott and Robert J. Valenza, 'Did Marlowe write half of *Henry VI, Part I*?', unpublished typescript (30 August 2013), p. 38.

[18] As Gardner, following Grierson, showed, Donne's 'silly old moralitie, | That as these linkes were knit, our love should bee' (ll. 5–6) alludes to the following passage in *Soliman and Perseda*: 'receiue this pretious Carcanet, | In signe, that as these linkes are interlaced, | So both our hearts are still combind in one' (TLN 755–7); and the 'lowd squeaking Cryer, | Well-pleas'd with one leane thread-bare groat, for hire, | May like a devill roare through every street' (ll. 55–7) recalls the crier whom Piston employs to find the lost chain (TLN 500–47) (see Grierson (ed.), *The Poems of John Donne*, 2 vols (Oxford, 1912), 2.78; Gardner (ed.), *John Donne: The Elegies and the Songs and Sonnets* (Oxford, 1965), p. 112). Roma Gill has agreed that 'The Bracelet' is 'almost certainly inspired' by *Soliman and Perseda* ('Musa Iocosa Mean: Thoughts on the Elegies', in *John Donne: Essays in Celebration*, ed. A. J. Smith (London, 1972), pp. 47–72, p. 66).

[19] Gardner (ed.), *John Donne*, p. 112

[20] Quoted from Kyd's first letter to Sir John Puckering, BL Harl. MS 6849, fols 218–19, printed by Freeman, *Thomas Kyd*, p. 181.

keeping of a dangerous document' and that 'The Bracelet' thus provides a piece of external evidence relating *Soliman and Perseda* to its author.[21] Much evidence thus militates for and little against Kyd's authorship of *Soliman and Perseda*.[22]

The title-pages of the early quartos mention neither an acting company nor a playhouse, and the play does not appear in Philip Henslowe's diary. Alfred Hart argued on the basis of 'inter-play borrowings' between *Soliman and Perseda* and a number of contemporary plays (including *Edward II*, *Arden of Faversham*, *The First Part of the Contention*, and *The True Tragedy of Richard Duke of York*) that it must at one point have belonged to the repertory of the Earl of Pembroke's Men.[23] Shakespeare was clearly familiar with the play, as instanced by his allusion to 'Basilisco' in *King John*.[24] The final lines include a compliment to the Queen—'sacred *Cynthias* friend' (TLN 2402)—which could suggest that the play was performed at court.[25] The printed text distinguishes between a main stage and a space above: the crier enters on the main stage through a '*doore*' (TLN 499), and Erastus is bound to a '*post*' (TLN 2024). In the upper acting space, Perseda, Basilisco, and Piston appear on the '*walles*' (TLN 2213) from which 'Perseda *comes downe to* Soliman' (TLN 2255) with them; earlier in the play the Lord Marshall takes the two witnesses to the '*tower top*' (TLN 2065) from which they are '*both tumbled downe*' (TLN 2074). A few stage directions appear to be missing:[26] at TLN 421, no exit is provided for Piston; Iulio enters at TLN 1056, janissaries at TLN 1218 and Death at TLN 2363, but none of these characters has an exit stage direction; and the drummer, mentioned at TLN 967, has neither an entrance nor an exit stage direction. '*Exeunt.*' at TLN 2361 seems redundant given the following line; and at TLN 1458, '*Exeunt, to the batel.*' implies the battle takes place offstage, but 'Phylippo *and* Cipris *are both slaine.*' (TLN 1459) may suggest that the combatants re-enter and die on stage. On the whole, however, most of the necessary stage directions are provided, and they are by no means incompatible with the conventions known from performance by professional

---

[21] Gardner (ed.), *John Donne*, p. 118.

[22] See also Lukas Erne, *Beyond 'The Spanish Tragedy': A Study of the Works of Thomas Kyd* (Manchester, 2001), pp. 160–2. Concerning the play's literary and dramatic interest and its relationship to its source, a novella in Henry Wotton's *A Courtlie Controuersie of Cupids Cautels* (1578), see Erne, *Beyond 'The Spanish Tragedy'*, pp. 168–202.

[23] See Alfred Hart, *Stolne and Surreptitious Copies: A Comparative Study of Shakespeare's Bad Quartos* (Melbourne, 1942), pp. 352–90. For a possible allusion to a performance of the play at the Swan Theatre, see Freeman, *Thomas Kyd*, pp. 156–7; for the 'Play of Erastus' (perhaps an alternative title for *Soliman and Perseda*), which was performed at Strasbourg by Thomas Sackville's company in 1597, see Martin Wiggins, *British Drama 1533–1642: A Catalogue: Volume II: 1567–1589* (Oxford, 2012), p. 406.

[24] See the Bastard's '"Knight, knight", good mother, Basilisco-like!' (1.1.244, quoted from A. R. Braunmuller (ed.), *King John*, The Oxford Shakespeare (Oxford, 1989)).

[25] For the play's conjectured date of 1588/89, see Erne, *Beyond 'The Spanish Tragedy'*, pp. 158–60.

[26] Absent exit stage directions are not uncommon in early modern theatrical manuscripts. See Eugene Giddens, *How to Read a Shakespearean Play Text* (Cambridge, 2011), p. 83.

companies.[27] Two marginal manuscript stage directions in an early modern hand in the only extant copy of the undated quarto indicate preparation for the stage, although it is impossible to say whether the preparation led to performance and, if it did, in what venue. At Soliman's exit at TLN 1372, when the Turkish emperor has promised Erastus he will 'see what pleasures and what sports, | My Minions and my Euenukes can deuise,' (TLN 1370–1), the first stage direction asks for 'the daunce | before Piston | enters'; and when Soliman has exited at lines TLN 1772–3, having announced he will 'go sit among my learned Euenukes, | And here them play, and see my minions dance', the second stage direction asks for 'the songe to | be sunge before | Basilisco | enters' (the second 'e' in 'before' is only partly visible because the page has been cropped).

The close textual relationship between the two early editions suggests that one was set up from the other. It is usually assumed that the edition of 1599 derives from the undated edition. The entry in the Stationers' Register of 20 November 1592 makes the publication of an edition soon after likely (though not certain). The words on the title-page of the second issue of the 1599 edition—'Newly corrected and amended.'—indicate that it supersedes an earlier edition, and the fact that the extant copy of the undated edition contains an instance of serious textual corruption absent from the 1599 edition (see below, pp. xviii–xix) may suggest that the added title-page announcement is correct. Moreover, the text of the two editions occasionally differs in ways which suggest that the one dated 1599 tries to make sense of misreadings in the undated one. For instance, whereas the undated edition enigmatically reads 'the big-bound Dane' (TLN 120), that of 1599 more sensibly has 'the bigbon'd Dane' (A3v). Similarly suggestive are variations in the name of Lucina's beloved: he is at first called 'Ferdinando' in stage direction and dialogue, but then variously 'Ferdinando' or 'Fernando'. At the point where the undated edition has the first occurrence of *'Fernando'* (TLN 741), the edition of 1599 reads *'Ferdinando'* (C4r), probably an attempt to remove what was perceived to be an anomaly. Most decisively, a printer's ornament used in both editions on the title-page shows clearly visible degradation in the edition of 1599 but not in the undated edition (see below, p. xx). External and internal evidence thus concur to suggest that the undated edition is the earlier of the two.

The undated edition is usually assumed to have been published soon after the play had been entered in the Stationers' Register. The STC dates the edition '1592?', and Freeman has written that 'conventionally it is assigned the date of the year of entry, 1592'.[28] Yet given that *Soliman and Perseda* was not

---

[27] Murray considered it 'improbable' that the play 'was ever performed in a public playhouse' and thought that the *'Mule'* (TLN 471)—alternatively referred to as an *'Asse'* (TLN 498)—would have been difficult to accommodate to the early modern professional stage (Murray (ed.), *The Tragedye of Solyman and Perseda*, p. xxi). But Alan C. Dessen and Leslie Thomson have shown that 'the *ass* . . . occasionally appears onstage' in early modern public plays (*A Dictionary of Stage Directions in English Drama, 1580–1642* (Cambridge, 1999), p. 16), and its presence thus affords no reason to doubt that *Soliman and Perseda* was performed.

[28] Freeman, *Thomas Kyd*, p. 154.

entered until 20 November 1592, the first edition may well not have appeared until 1593. A survey of plays entered in the Stationers' Register between 1580 and 1610 shows that, according to the imprint, not a single play entered later in the year than *Soliman and Perseda* was published before the end of the year. Plays entered in the Stationers' Register late in the year and published before the end of the year include *Richard III* (entered 20 October 1597), Thomas Dekker and Thomas Middleton's *1 The Honest Whore* (9 November 1604), *Wily Beguiled* (12 November 1606), and *A Warning for Fair Women* (17 November 1599). By contrast, quite a number of plays were entered earlier in the year than *Soliman and Perseda* but were not published until the following year according to the imprint: Middleton's *A Trick to Catch the Old One* (entered 7 October 1607), and *The Family of Love* (12 October 1607), *2 Return from Parnassus* (16 October 1605), Samuel Daniel's *Cleopatra* (19 October 1593), *The Merry Devil of Edmonton* (22 October 1607), and Ben Jonson's *Sejanus* (2 November 1604). *Jack Straw*, entered on 23 October 1593, was published in 1593 according to the title-page and in 1594 according to the colophon. On the other hand, as will be shown below (see pp. xvii–xviii), there is no reason to believe that the printing office in which the first edition of *Soliman and Perseda* was set was particularly busy late in 1592, so it is possible that the play could have been published before the end of December. The year of publication of the first edition of *Soliman and Perseda*, 1592 or 1593, thus remains conjectural.

The text of the undated edition was printed on extra-large paper that had been cut in two.[29] This means the chain lines are perpendicular, with four pages of type on either side of a sheet.[30] Following R. B. McKerrow, who considered the sheet as originally manufactured decisive for a book's format, W. W. Greg referred to the edition as a '(4°-form) 8°', and Philip Gaskell

[29] This method may have been an expedient for clearing excess stock of the larger paper. Freeman has called such paper cut in two 'quite uncommon in this period' ('The Printing of *The Spanish tragedy*', 198), but in fact a number of other books published by Edward White are large-paper quartos, including several playbooks: *A Merry Jest of Robin Hood and of His Life* (1590, STC 13692), *The Spanish Tragedy* (1592, STC 15086; and 1594, STC 15087), Richard Edwards's *The paradice of dainty deuises* (1596, STC 7521), *Soliman and Perseda* (1599, STC 22895), *The Wit of a Woman* (1604, STC 25868), *1 Tamburlaine* (1605, STC 17428), *A briefe summe of the treason intended against the King and state* (1606, STC 20960), and *Titus Andronicus* (1611, STC 22330). Owing to cropping, the watermark in the only extant copy of Q1 *Soliman and Perseda* is only partly visible (see the head of A3, A4, E3, E4, G3, G4 and I2). A similar watermark is visible in the only extant copy of the first edition of *The Spanish Tragedy* (printed by the same printer, Allde, for the same publisher, White, around the same time), and since the copy of *The Spanish Tragedy* has been less cropped than that of *Soliman and Perseda*, more of the watermark is visible in the former book (see, in particular, C4; it resembles the shape of a wine glass with three loops connecting the brim on either side). Briquet's dictionary of watermarks does not contain an exact match (see C. M. Briquet, *Les Filigranes: Dictionnaire historique des marques du papier dès leur apparition vers 1282 jusqu'en 1600*, ed. Allan Stevenson, 4 vols (Amsterdam, 1968)), and there is no close resemblance to Briquet 14036 (see Freeman, 'The Printing of *The Spanish tragedy*', 198–9).

[30] As W. W. Greg has commented, 'In the only known copy the fore-edge of one leaf (H4) has escaped trimming and shows a torn and not a deckle edge, thus proving that the paper was made in sheets of double size' (*Bibliography*, 1.186).

called the format 'octavo-in-fours'.[31] Yet G. T. Tanselle, in a comprehensive examination of the concept of format, has commented on 'the illogicality of making chainline direction an essential determinant of format' and has argued that books like the undated edition of *Soliman and Perseda* are 'simply quartos, printed throughout from four-page formes'.[32] The present introduction follows Tanselle in considering the first edition of *Soliman and Perseda* a quarto (henceforth referred to as Q1, and the 1599 edition as Q2).[33]

Soliman and Perseda was published by Edward White, a bookseller in London from 1577 to 1612 who kept a shop near the little North door of Paul's Churchyard throughout his career.[34] He published close to 200 titles, covering a wide generic range, from theology—including a volume of Calvin's sermons in 1578 (STC 4432)—via literature and practical handbooks to ballads and other ephemera. Among his bestsellers were Thomas Lupton's *A thousand notable things of sundry sortes* (STC 16956–9.5) and T. C.'s (Thomas Cartwright's?) *An Hospitall for the diseased* (STC 4305–8), of which he published at least seven editions each. Among his literary titles, he repeatedly published texts by Robert Greene, notably *Morando, the tritameron of loue* in 1583 (STC 12276), *Euphues his censure to Philautus* in 1587 (STC 12239), *Perimedes the blacke-smith* in 1588 (STC 12295), and *Philomela* in 1592 (STC 12296). He also published the poetical miscellany *The paradice of dainty deuises* (1585, STC 7520) and the prose *History of Doctor Faustus* (1592, STC 10711).

White was particularly active as an early publisher of professional drama. In the 1580s, only a handful of professional plays appeared in print, among which was the anonymous *Rare Triumphs of Love and Fortune* (1589, STC 24286), published by White.[35] In the last decade of the sixteenth century, as the publication of professional plays became more frequent, White issued several other plays, *Arden of Faversham* and *The Spanish Tragedy*, both in 1592, *Soliman and Perseda* in 1592/3, then Christopher Marlowe's *Massacre at Paris* and Robert Greene's *Friar Bacon and Friar Bungay* in 1594. It has recently been argued that he also had a hand in the publication of the first quarto of *Titus Andronicus* (1594, STC 22328).[36] Still in 1594, White also acquired the

[31] See McKerrow, *An Introduction to Bibliography*, pp. 164–74, and Philip Gaskell, *A New Introduction to Bibliography* (Oxford, 1972), p. 106. See also Fredson Bowers, *Principles of Bibliographical Description* (Princeton, NJ, 1949), pp. 193–4.

[32] Tanselle, 'The Concept of Format', *Studies in Bibliography*, 53 (2000), 67–115, 89, 90.

[33] The chainlines of the second quarto, like those of the first, are perpendicular, suggesting that it, too, was printed on extra-large paper that had been cut in half.

[34] See Peter W. M. Blayney's map of 'Paul's Churchyard & Environs' in A. W. Pollard and G. R. Redgrave, *A Short-Title Catalogue of Books Printed in England, Scotland and Ireland and of English Books Printed Abroad, 1475–1640*, 2nd edn, revised and enlarged by W. A. Jackson, F. S. Ferguson, and Katharine F. Pantzer, 3 vols (London: Bibliographical Society, 1976–91), vol. 3, facing p. 243.

[35] The other professional plays first published in the 1580s are John Lyly's *Campaspe* and *Sapho and Phao* (1584, STC 17047.5 and 17086), George Peele's *The Arraignment of Paris* (1584, STC 19530) and Robert Wilson's *The Three Ladies of London* (1584, STC 25784).

[36] See Lukas Erne, *Shakespeare and the Book Trade* (Cambridge, 2013), pp. 139–40.

rights in the anonymous *King Leir* by substitution in the Stationers' Register of his name for that of Adam Islip, to whom it was entered on 14 May.[37] Its earliest extant edition is dated 1605 (published by John Wright), but given the low number of surviving copies of White's early playbooks, it is possible that he also published an edition of *King Leir* in or shortly after 1594.

Arden of Faversham (1599), *The Spanish Tragedy* (1594), *Soliman and Perseda* (1599), and *Titus Andronicus* (1600) are all second editions published by White, who went on to add a third of *Titus* (1611). Further plays joined White's list: he published the first edition of Thomas Dekker's *Satiromastix* (1602) and the fourth edition of Christopher Marlowe's *Tamburlaine, Part I* (1605) and *Part II* (1606). All in all, White published fifteen editions of ten plays, making him a regular publisher of professional plays. Like *Soliman and Perseda*, most of the plays White published appeared anonymously. Thirteen of the fifteen editions White published named no author, the two exceptions being *Friar Bacon and Friar Bungay*, 'Made by *Robert Greene* Maister of Arts', and *Satiromastix*, 'By *Thomas Dekker*'. That the early editions of *Soliman and Perseda* were published anonymously is accordingly unexceptional.

White seems to have published *Arden of Faversham*, *The Spanish Tragedy*, and *Soliman and Perseda* (all printed by Allde) in the space of a few months. *Arden* was entered to White on 3 April 1592 and appeared in an edition printed by Allde for White dated 1592. *The Spanish Tragedy* was entered on 6 October, not to White but to Abel Jeffes, who may have been on the point of publishing an edition of the play or, more likely, had already done so earlier in the year.[38] Although he did not own the rights in the play, White likewise published an edition of *The Spanish Tragedy*, perhaps in retaliation for a surreptitious edition of *Arden of Faversham* published by Jeffes. The Stationers' Company, according to the minutes of 18 December 1592 from the Court Book of the Company, went on to punish both Jeffes and White for the infringement of each other's rights:

Whereas Edward white and Abell Ieffes haue eche of them offendyd. Viz Edw White in havinge printed the spanish tragedie belonging to Abell Ieffes/ and Abell Ieffes in having printed the tragedie of arden of kent belonginge to Edw white: yt is agreed that all the bookes of eche ympression shalbe as confiscated and forfayted accordinge to thordonnances, disposed to thuse of the poore of the companye for that eche of them hath seu'ally transgressed the ordonances in the seid impressions/[39]

A later entry in the Wardens' account suggests that the publishers were permitted to buy back and resell their confiscated books.[40] No copy of Jeffes's surreptitious edition of *Arden* is extant, whereas White's authorized edition has survived. Of *The Spanish Tragedy*, conversely, the authorized edition, by Jeffes, has perished, whereas White's surreptitious edition survives, in the

[37] See Greg, *Bibliography*, 1.11.

[38] W. W. Greg and D. Nichol Smith (eds), *The Spanish Tragedy (1592)*, The Malone Society Reprints (Oxford, 1948 (1949)), p. ix.

[39] W. W. Greg and E. Boswell (eds), *Records of the Court of the Stationers' Company, 1576 to 1602, from Register B* (London, 1930), p. 44.

[40] See Greg and Nichol Smith (eds), *The Spanish Tragedy (1592)*, pp. x–xi.

form of a single copy now at the British Library. The title-page claims that it has been 'Newly corrected and amended of such grosse faults as passed in the first impression', suggesting that White may have had access to a different manuscript from the one used in setting Jeffes's edition.[41]

If White obtained an independent manuscript of *The Spanish Tragedy* late in 1592, it may be significant that he entered *Soliman and Perseda* at about the same time, on 20 November. The two plays are closely related: not only were both, in all likelihood, written by Kyd, but *Soliman and Perseda* constitutes a full-length treatment of the play-within-the-play of the last act of *The Spanish Tragedy*. It seems unlikely that the two plays were owned by the same company: *The Spanish Tragedy* had a successful run of performances by the Lord Strange's Men in 1592 as recorded in Henslowe's diary.[42] *Soliman and Perseda*, by contrast, is never mentioned by Henslowe and is more likely to have been owned by the Earl of Pembroke's Men (see above, p. xi). It is possible to speculate that the reason why the two plays were published by the same stationer around the same time may be that Kyd sold White the manuscripts. It is also worthwhile remembering that *Arden of Faversham*, entered earlier in the same year, has repeatedly been ascribed to Kyd, most recently by Brian Vickers.[43] Furthermore, *Arden of Faversham* and *Soliman and Perseda* share a distinctive feature unique to play texts of this period, a high number of stage directions starting with '*Then*', which may encourage further speculation in favour of common authorship.[44] It is impossible to recover what events or processes led to the appearance in print of *Arden of Faversham*, *The Spanish Tragedy*, and *Soliman and Perseda*, but the quick succession of the three plays, published by White and printed by Allde, is intriguing.

Allde was a printer in London from 1584, when he was made free of the Stationers' Company, to 1627, the year of his death. He has been described by McKerrow as 'a typical commercial man with no pretensions to be anything else [who] was never particularly prominent in the trade', 'a fairly competent commercial printer, who having inherited a small but sound business from his

[41] By 1594, White and Jeffes's dispute seems to have been settled, since they did joint business on that year's edition of *The Spanish Tragedy*, which, according to the title-page, was 'Printed by Abell Ieffes' and 'to be sold by Edward White'.

[42] See R. A. Foakes (ed.), *Henslowe's Diary*, 2nd edn (Cambridge, 2002), pp. 16–19.

[43] See Vickers, 'Thomas Kyd, Secret Sharer'. The argument for Kyd's authorship of *Arden of Faversham* has been rejected by Arthur F. Kinney ('Authoring *Arden of Faversham*', in Hugh Craig and Arthur F. Kinney, *Shakespeare, Computers, and the Mystery of Authorship* (Cambridge, 2009), pp. 78–99) and MacDonald P. Jackson ('Parallels and Poetry: Shakespeare, Kyd, and *Arden of Faversham*', *Medieval and Renaissance Drama in England*, 23 (2010), 17–33). They argue instead for Shakespeare's part-authorship of *Arden* (see Kinney, 'Authoring *Arden of Faversham*', and Jackson, 'Shakespeare and the Quarrel Scene in *Arden of Faversham*', *Shakespeare Quarterly*, 57 (2006), 249–93).

[44] For *Soliman and Perseda*, see TLN 331, 360–1, 651, 654, 976–7, 979, 999, 1109, 1331, 1623, 1698, 1819, 2039, 2056, 2065, 2074, 2085, 2148, 2152, 2255–6, 2261, 2275, 2283, 2321 and 2362. Stage directions using '*Then*' occur in *Arden* on signatures B2ʳ, B3ʳ, B3ᵛ, D1ʳ, D1ᵛ, F1ᵛ, F2ʳ (2×), G1ʳ, G2ᵛ, I1ʳ (2×), I1ᵛ, I2ᵛ, and I3ʳ. Note, however, that entrance stage directions in *Arden of Faversham* start with '*Here*' (e.g. '*Here enters Clarke.*', B1ᵛ), a feature not shared with *Soliman and Perseda*.

father, gradually enlarged it, worked it for nearly fifty years, and, dying, left it to his widow.'[45] He is known to have 'Imprinted at the long Shop adioyning vnto Saint Mildreds Church in the Pultrie' from 1584 to at least 1588. By 1590, he resided 'without Cripplegate at the signe of the guilded Cuppe', and in 1597, he was 'dwelling in Aldersgate street over against the Pump'.[46] In the course of his career, he was involved in the production of more than 700 titles mentioned in the *Short-Title Catalogue*.[47] He started as a small printer–publisher (1584–90), but from 1591 was chiefly active as a trade printer who worked for others. According to McKerrow, 'Allde seems to have printed for some 86 different booksellers, for some 55 of which he only produced a single book.' Some of his professional relationships were long-lived, however, in particular with Edward White, the publisher of *Soliman and Perseda*, and his son, Edward White, junior, who was active as a bookseller from 1605 to 1624. He printed more than fifty titles for father and son between 1587 and 1621.[48]

Estimates of the productivity of Allde's printing house are hampered by what must be considerable loss rates. Most of Allde's books are, as McKerrow pointed out, 'exceedingly scarce . . . probably [as] a result of the popular and ephemeral nature of a great part of his output'. McKerrow added that many books printed by Allde (and they include Q1 *Soliman and Perseda*) 'are only known from single copies', that some 'which he entered in the Stationers' Register and probably printed are not now known to exist', and that 'of others editions have certainly vanished'.[49] What further complicates an assessment of Allde's printing output is the absence of a publication date from quite a number of his title-pages. In 1592, Allde printed *Arden of Faversham* (STC 733, 9¼ sheets), *Articles to be enquired of* (STC 10268.2, 1½ sheets), *A godly sermon* by William Fisher (STC 10919, 4 sheets), *De fide . . . Per E.H.* (STC 12563, 4⅜ sheets), *The Spanish tragedie* (STC 15086, 10½ sheets), *The new attractiue* (STC 18649, 19½ sheets), *A golden chaine* (STC 19660, 20⅞ sheets), and *To the seminarye priests lately come ouer . . . by Richard Briflowe* (STC 22185, 4½ sheets). According to the STC, he also printed *The trumpet of the soule . . . By Henry Smyth* (STC 22707, 1¼ sheets); and *Greenes vision* (STC 12261, 8 sheets) and *Newes from Scotland* (STC 10841a, 3¾ sheets), both conjecturally dated 1592; and shared the printing of Robert Greene's *Philomela*, with Robert Bourne (STC 12296, 9½ sheets, of which 4½ are by Allde), Humfrey Barwick's *A breefe discourse,* with Richard Oliffe, conjecturally dated 1592 (STC 1542, 10½ sheets), and Hugh Broughton's *An apologie in briefe assertions*, with Thomas East and Richard Watkins (STC 3845, 11¼ sheets).[50] Only

[45] R. B. McKerrow, 'Edward Allde As a Typical Trade Printer', *The Library* 4th ser., 10 (1929–30), 121–62, 123, 124.

[46] Quotations are from McKerrow, 'Edward Allde', 128.

[47] For Allde, see also Ian Gadd, 'Allde [Alldee], Edward (1555×63–1627), printer', *Oxford Dictionary of National Biography*, Oxford, 2004 <http://www.oxforddnb.com/view/article/363, accessed 31 July 2013>.

[48] See McKerrow, 'Edward Allde', 138. See also Pollard and Redgrave, *A Short-Title Catalogue*, 3.2–3.

[49] McKerrow, 'Edward Allde', 132; see also p. 141.

[50] The conjectural date of STC 1542 is changed from '1594?' to '1592?' in volume 3.

one book dated 1593 was certainly printed by Allde: Thomas Hyll's *The profitable arte of gardening* (STC 13496, 32 sheets). A second book, *Tarltons newes out of purgatorie* (STC 23685a, 7 sheets), is conjecturally dated 1593 by the STC (vol. 3). If this is correct, and if the 8½ sheets of *Soliman and Perseda* are discounted, the total amounts to 88 sheets, plus a share of the 21¾ sheets of STC 1542 and 3845, so close to 100 sheets (roughly the equivalent of 800 quarto pages) printed by Allde in 1592; and to 39 sheets (*c.*312 quarto pages) printed by him in 1593.

These totals are quite low compared to the output of most contemporary printers. McKerrow suggested that Allde's books may have been 'much more numerous than we are aware of' or that 'he may have done a good deal of printing that was not book-printing at all . . . of which only a minute proportion would survive'.[51] Both suggestions may partly account for the relative scarcity of material that can now be assigned to Allde's printing house. Nonetheless, it seems clear that Allde's printing business in 1592 and 1593 may have been relatively small.[52]

Allde had printed several plays before *Soliman and Perseda*: the third quarto of Thomas Preston's *Cambises* in 1585 (STC 20287.5), the third quarto of Ulpian Fulwel's *Like Will to Like* in 1587 (STC 11474), the first quarto of the anonymous *The Rare Triumphs of Love and Fortune* in 1589 (STC 24286), the third quarto of Thomas Norton and Thomas Sackville's *Gorboduc* in 1590 (STC 17029), and the first quartos of *Arden of Faversham* (STC 733) and *The Spanish Tragedy* (STC 15086) in 1592. When printing *Soliman and Perseda*, Allde and his workmen did not produce a particularly clean text (see the Appendix for a list of erroneous and doubtful readings). The most serious textual error in Q1 *Soliman and Perseda* is that a line accidentally appears at the head of E2^r (TLN 1180) that in fact belongs at the head of E3^r (before TLN 1252) (this was corrected in Q2).[53] What bears witness to this error is

---

[51] McKerrow, 'Edward Allde', 144–5.

[52] Two apprentices joined Allde's printing business in 1594, Thomas Nycols on 1 May and Godfrey Smyth on 4 November (Arber, *Transcript*, 2.191, 199), but it is not clear whether he had a single apprentice in late 1592 and 1593: John Munnes, who had started his apprenticeship with Edward Allde's father John in 1581 and continued it with Edward Allde from 4 August 1589, was made free on 5 June 1592 (Arber, *Transcript*, 2.107, 162, 710). Allde's only other apprentice from this period mentioned in the records of the Stationers' Company is 'John ffishwick sonne of GREGORYE FFISHWICK of LICHFEILD'. The entry recording his apprenticeship, which started on 30 March 1589, is crossed out and a marginal note reads: 'This apprentice is dead' (Arber, *Transcript*, 2.163). The date of his death is not recorded.

[53] Freeman argued that the correction happened during the printing of Q1: 'the extant example of *1592* is of an early uncorrected state of the printing, and *1599* is set up from a copy of the lost later state'. This theory, he argued, 'would explain how the *1599* compositor happened to catch the error, as it is rather improbable that anyone would adduce the correction at seven years' distance without consulting the original copy again' (*Thomas Kyd*, p. 155 n. 3). But the 1599 compositor did not need the original copy to notice the error: the failure of the catchwords on E1^v and E2^v to correspond to the first words on E2^r and E3^r would have alerted him to the problem, and since the catchword on E1^v corresponds to the first word of the second line on E2^r, and the catchword on E2^v to the first word of the first line on E2^r, it would have been easy to reconstruct what happened. Nor does Freeman's theory account for the fact that the line at the top of E2^v in Q1 appears at the foot of E2^r in Q2.

not only that the two passages do not make sense in their Q1 arrangement but that the catchwords at the foot of E1ᵛ and E2ᵛ fail to correspond to the first word on the following page. How exactly the line came to be misplaced is difficult to fathom. It might have resulted from an overflow problem when it was attempted to adjust the number of lines per page so as to keep it at the usual thirty-seven lines.[54] Once the pages of sheet E (at least up to E4ʳ) had been set, with the line that came to be misplaced originally at the head of E3ʳ (as the catchword at the foot of E2ᵛ suggests), a compositor may have realized that E3ʳ amounted to thirty-eight lines (with no blank line). If E3ʳ or E4ᵛ had contained any blank lines, it would have been easiest to remove the last line of E3ʳ and to make space for it at the head of E3ᵛ by removing the blank line, but since neither page contains any blank lines, this would not have been an option. Therefore, the first line of E3ʳ was removed with the idea of finding space for it on the preceding page (which does contain a blank line) but then accidentally placed at the head of E2ʳ. Adrian Weiss has documented what may be a similar 'pull-back' of a part-line from the first line of a page to the last line of the preceding page in *A Faire Quarrell* (1617).[55] As in *Soliman and Perseda*, the compositor forgot to correct the catchword after the pull-back, but at least he put the part-line in the right place, whereas Allde's compositor did not.[56]

Allde used four printer's ornaments in *Soliman and Perseda*, two of which he used regularly. The one appearing before the head-title on A2ʳ has been described as 'The sun rising clear of clouds in centre: cherubs at sides' by McKerrow, who believed that it 'is probably the ornament of which Allde made most frequent use'. He added that 'it seems not impossible that it was an attempt at a punning device having reference to Allde's name, taken as equivalent to spelt "All-day"'.[57] Allde used it twice in 1591, three times each in 1592 and 1593 (excluding *Soliman and Perseda*), and kept employing it throughout his career.[58] The other ornament in *Soliman and Perseda* that

[54] A2ᵛ contains thirty-six lines (including one that is blank), but all the following pages through to the penultimate one (A3ʳ to I2ʳ) have thirty-seven lines (including occasional blank lines), not counting headline or catchword.

[55] See Adrian Weiss, 'Casting Compositors, Foul Cases, and Skeletons: Printing in Middleton's Age', in *Thomas Middleton and Early Modern Textual Culture: A Companion to the Collected Works*, gen. eds, Gary Taylor and John Lavagnino (Oxford, 2007), pp. 195–225, p. 216.

[56] Freeman advanced a different theory regarding the origin of the misplaced line, arguing that 'what actually happened was probably that the type fell out of the case [i.e., chase] from the top of E3ʳ . . . and was accidentally replaced in the corresponding position in the other forme' (*Thomas Kyd*, p. 155 n. 3).

[57] McKerrow, 'Edward Allde', 149.

[58] The ornament has been identified in the following books printed by Allde: 1591: STC 6818, 10919, 12261, 19876, 22185; 1593: STC 13496; 1596: STC 5803, 6820, 18007; 1597: STC 12906, 17673; 1599: STC 3470, 22895; 1601: STC 17547; 1602: STC 12197, 16754, 23679; 1603: STC 14354; 1605: STC 3020.5, 18589, 25967; 1606: STC 23464; 1607: STC 20400, 21368, 24063; 1608: STC 21368.5, 21368.7, 22795.7, 24053.5; 1609: STC 18108, 25022; 1610: STC 20401, 20768; 1611: STC 22992.7; 1612: STC 3708, 25915; 1613: STC 3709; 1614: STC 18274; 1616: STC 13567, 21494.5; 1621: STC 23793.

Allde frequently used—a 'Winged torso of somewhat Mongolian aspect hold-ing ends of volutes'—appears on I2ᵛ, between the end of the text ('*FINIS*') and the colophon. McKerrow wrote that it can be 'Found from 1593',[59] but it already appears in fact in Hugh Broughton's *An apologie in briefe asser-tions* (STC 3845), dated 1592, and in *Greenes vision* (STC 12261), which is undated but assigned to 1592 by the STC.[60] The two remaining ornaments in *Soliman and Perseda* appear on the title-page. The head-compartment, not mentioned by McKerrow, appears in titles in a few other books printed by Allde in the 1590s, among them the first quarto of *The Spanish Tragedy*.[61] Finally, the 'circular ornament of conventional foliage within a triple rule' between title and imprint,[62] appears occasionally in Allde's books from 1592 to 1616, though only rarely after 1603.[63] The reason why Allde did not use it more frequently may be that it suffered clearly visible degradation from about 1597 (STC 12906), when a crack in the outer rule first became visible that grew substantially bigger through subsequent use. Three of the ornaments used in *Soliman and Perseda* were in regular use by Allde from 1592, the fourth from 1591.

In all pre-1592 playbooks printed by Allde as well as in *Arden of Faversham*, the dialogue is in black letter, with roman and italics reserved for stage direc-tions, speech headings, and paratext.[64] *The Spanish Tragedy* and *Soliman and Perseda*, by contrast, have most of the dialogue set in pica roman, with ital-ics reserved for part of the stage directions, speech headings, and names and

---

[59] McKerrow, 'Edward Allde', 149.

[60] For this ornament, see the following of Allde's books: 1592: STC 3845, 12261; 1593: STC 13496; 1596: STC 18007; 1597: STC 17673; 1599: STC 12995, 20121.5, 20861, 21301, 22895, 24216; 1601: STC 2759.5; 1605: STC 7078, 18589; 1606: STC 22881.5; 1607: STC 18532; 1608: STC 21368.7, 23679.5, 24053.5; 1610: STC 4307.5, 13159, 20768; 1611: STC 6890; 1613: STC 25602; 1614: STC 18274; 1615: STC 18720; 1626: STC 21551.7.

[61] 1592: STC 15086; 1595: STC 23401.5; 1596: STC 6820; 1597: STC 17673; 1599: STC 20121.5, 22895.

[62] McKerrow, 'Edward Allde', p. 158.

[63] 1592: STC 1542, 12261; 1593: STC 13496; 1596: STC 6820; 1597: STC 12906; 1599: STC 22895; 1603: STC 14354; 1615: STC 10275.3; 1616: STC 10275.7. This ornament is listed in Henry R. Plomer, *English Printers' Ornaments* (London, 1924), number 93. At least one other ornament of similar size and related design (49.5 mm instead of 52 mm, accord-ing to McKerrow ('Edward Allde', 158)), owned by Richard Bradock, was in circulation (see Blayney, *The Texts of 'King Lear' and Their Origins: Volume 1, Nicholas Okes and the First Quarto* (Cambridge, 1982), p. 469). It appears, for instance, on the title-page of the first quarto of Marlowe's *Edward II* (STC 17437) and at the foot of the last page of the first quarto of Shakespeare's *A Midsummer Night's Dream* (STC 22302). Confusingly, the ornament appear-ing in STC 25840 (1613), on C3ᵛ, printed by Edward Allde and John Beale according to STC, is *not* the one owned by Allde but probably Bradock's. Yet another ornament of almost exactly the same size as Allde's (51 mm), though with a different design, appears in the 1607 edition of Shakespeare's *The Rape of Lucrece* (STC 22349, A3ᵛ), printed by Nicholas Okes (see Blayney, *The Texts of 'King Lear'*, pp. 444, 469).

[64] For playbooks and the cultural meaning of black letter, see Zachary Lesser, 'Typographic Nostalgia: Play-Reading, Popularity, and the Meanings of Black Letter', in *The Book of the Play: Playwrights, Stationers, and Readers in Early Modern England*, ed. Marta Straznicky (Amherst, MA, 2006), pp. 99–126.

passages in foreign languages in the dialogue text.[65] The printing conventions adopted in *The Spanish Tragedy* and *Soliman and Perseda* are thus similar but not identical: in *The Spanish Tragedy*, stage directions are in roman except for names and the words 'Exit' and 'Exeunt', which are usually in italics. In *Soliman and Perseda*, stage directions are mostly in italics, except for names, which are in roman.[66]

Arthur Freeman has identified another printing convention which markedly differs in *The Spanish Tragedy* and *Soliman and Perseda*, namely that of overrunning lines, which are turned up or down. *The Spanish Tragedy* has ten such lines,[67] whereas *Soliman and Perseda* has sixteen.[68] Of the latter, three had to be turned up by necessity (TLN 389, B3ʳ; TLN 503, B4ᵛ; TLN 1996, H1ʳ) and four down by necessity (TLN 150, A4ʳ; TLN 248, B1ʳ; TLN 277, B1ᵛ; TLN 2018, H1ʳ), but the remaining nine lines, where the compositor(s) could choose, are all turned down (TLN 273, B1ᵛ; TLN 286, B1ᵛ; TLN 317, B2ʳ; TLN 486, B4ᵛ; TLN 1087, D4ᵛ; TLN 1510, F2ᵛ; TLN 1945, G4ʳ; TLN 2197, H3ᵛ; TLN 2310, I1ʳ), 'a complex process, requiring reservation of the overflow, and atypical.'[69] The evidence leads Freeman to argue that the two texts were not set by the same compositors.

Conventions of italicization, punctuation, and placement of stage directions are on the whole consistent, with a few exceptions.[70] Unusually, three signings of leaves are partly in italics: 'D *3*', 'G *3*', and '*I* 2'. At TLN 2064 occurs an isolated instance of continuous printing of two speeches (cf. e.g. TLN 2134–5). The text contains no act and scene division except for 'Actus primus.' (TLN 18). In the catchwords, some variations are noticeable—'*Manet.*' / '*Manet*' (B1ᵛ–B2ʳ), 'Be-' / 'Beside' (B4ʳ⁻ᵛ), '*Fer-*' / '*Ferdinando*' (C3ᵛ–C4ʳ), '*Basi.*' / '*Bas.*' (F1ᵛ–F2ʳ), '*Per.* / *Perse.*' (H2ʳ⁻ᵛ), and '*Piston*' / '*Piston.*' (H2ᵛ–H3ʳ)—apart from those resulting from the misplaced line on E2r (see above, pp. xviii–xix). Spacing around punctuation is irregular throughout, with variations occuring within the same page and even the same line (e.g. TLN 369). Most frequently,

[65] The italicization of names is inconsistent. See 'Mulcibers' (TLN 280, B1ᵛ), 'Venus' (TLN 298, B2ʳ), 'Mars' (TLN 778, C4ᵛ), 'Basiliscos' (TLN 1495, F2ʳ), 'Erastus' (TLN 1560, F3ʳ), 'Basiliscoes' (TLN 1788, G2ʳ), 'Basilisco' (TLN 1800, G2ʳ), 'Erastus' (TLN 2165, H3ʳ), 'Alcides' (TLN 2167, H3ʳ), 'Hercules' (TLN 2167, H3ʳ), 'Pryam' (TLN 2169, H3ʳ), 'Soliman' (TLN 2239, H4ʳ). Also inconsistently italicized are 'Mahomet'; 'Cypris' (in 'Prince of Cypris'); 'Loue', 'Fortune' and 'Death'; the names of saints; and place names.

[66] Absolute consistency is not attained. The following (parts of) stage directions are exceptionally printed in roman: 'Laying his hand vpon his sword.' (TLN 240, B1ʳ), 'Ladies' (TLN 1415, F1ʳ), 'to the batel' (TLN 1458, F1ʳ), and 'with' (TLN 2196, H3ᵛ). The following names in stage directions are exceptionally in italics, not in roman: '*Cipris*' (TLN 169, A4ʳ), '*Cryer*' (TLN 499, B4ᵛ), '*Cypres*' (TLN 1444, F1ᵛ), '*S*oliman' (TLN 2362, I2ʳ), '*Loue*' (TLN 2394, I2ᵛ), and '*Fortune*' (TLN 2398, I2ᵛ).

[67] See Freeman, 'The Printing of *The Spanish tragedy*', 197–8.

[68] An additional such line may have been avoided at TLN 156–7 due to lack of space in the adjacent lines.

[69] Freeman, 'The Printing of *The Spanish tragedy*', 198. TLN 2197 would look quite awkward if turned up following and beneath stage directions, but it would fit. The present details of overflowing lines in *Soliman and Perseda* differ slightly from Freeman's, but the basic point remains the same.

[70] For stage directions that are exceptionally printed in roman, see footnote 66.

commas have no spaces around them, but sometimes they are followed by one (e.g. TLN 285) or have one on either side (e.g. TLN 286). Full stops are variously followed but not preceded by a space (e.g. TLN 45), preceded and followed by a space (e.g. TLN 820), or neither preceded nor followed by a space (e.g. TLN 252). Question marks are usually preceded by a space (e.g. TLN 877) but sometimes not (e.g. TLN 738).[71] And colons are usually preceded by a space (e.g. TLN 824), but not consistently so (e.g. TLN 1437).

Speech headings show some variations. Erastus, for instance, is usually 'E*rast.*' (or, owing to type shortage, 'E*rast.*'), but there are also occurrences of '*Era.*' (TLN 929, 1710, 1966), '*Erastus.*' (TLN 532, 534), and '*Eras.*' (1980). The two witnesses at Erastus' trial are variously referred to as '*Witnesses.*' (TLN 1977), '*Witnesse*' (TLN 1981), '*Witn.*' (TLN 1991), '*The other wit.*' (TLN 1997), '*1.Wit.*' (TLN 2015), '*2.Wit.*' (TLN 2016), '*1.Witn.*' (TLN 2064), and '*2.Witn.*' (TLN 2064). Three of these speech headings— '*Witnesse*', '*Witn.*', and '*The other wit.*'—are inconveniently vague from the point of view of performance, which may suggest that the manuscript from which the first quarto was set up was an authorial draft. Permissive formulations in stage directions such as '*all the Knights*' (TLN 170), '*with other Souldiours*' (TLN 1431–2), and '*his Souldiers*' (TLN 1442) may corroborate such a hypothesis.

Variations in the speech headings of two characters look at first like candidates for the identification of different compositors: for the character of Perseda, '*Per.*' is used consistently on sheet A (five times), but in her subsequent appearances, '*Perse.*' is favoured, of which there are forty occurrences from C4^v to G1^r, with only four exceptional uses of '*Per.*', two on D1^r (with one occurrence of '*Perse.*' on the same page), and, in tight lines, one each on F1^r and F4^r. From G1^r onwards, however, '*Per.*' and '*Perse.*' appear interchangeably, in the same forme and even on the same page. Only on H4^r is the speech heading consistently '*Per.*' (seven times). For the character of Basilisco, '*Basi.*' is used on B1^r and B2^r but then gives way to '*Bas.*' for the rest of sheet B in either forme. '*Bas.*' recurs on C4^r, C4^v, and D1^r, and '*Basi.*' reappears on E1^v and E2^r. But any expectation of a consistent pattern is thwarted by sheets F, G, and H, where both speech headings appear, occasionally even on the same page (G2^v, H2^v). If other compositorial preferences coincided with the '*Per.*' / '*Perse.*' or the '*Bas.*' / '*Basi.*' patterns in the early sheets, these might nonetheless be leads worth pursuing, but, as will be seen, little serves to corroborate them.

Another marked shift in compositorial preference that does not coincide with either of those noted in the speech headings concerns the italicization of place names. They are mostly in roman, but fourteen are in italics. Of these, four are isolated occurences on pages where other place names are in roman (F3^r, G2^r, H1^r, and H3^v), but the other ten appear successively on C1^v ('*Rhodes*', '*Rhodes*', '*Persia*', '*Russian*', '*Rhodes*') and C2^r ('*Persea*', '*Polonia*', '*Persea*', '*Rhodes*', '*Persea*'), two pages with no place names in roman.[72] On

---

[71] A considerable number of question marks were set in italics (e.g. TLN 793), not in roman.

[72] As Richard Proudfoot has pointed out privately, the place names in italic on C1^v–2^r are all in the same scene, so copy usage could be involved.

B1^r, seven place names appear in roman, following which no other place names appear until C1^v, when they are in italics. Following C1^v and C2^r, place names revert to roman, two on C2^v, one on C3^v, and so on.

Like the marked changes in speech headings, those in place names do not obviously correlate with other compositorial preferences. Throughout the text, the spelling 'do' is preferred, with only a few occasional occurrences of 'doe' or 'doo'. The endings '-ie' and '-y[e]' co-exist throughout, with no discernible pattern in sheets B to H and with a preference for '-y[e]' in sheets A and I, which, however, is probably too slight to be of significance. Nor do the spellings 'here' and 'heer[e]', which co-exist with no clear pattern, suggest distinct preferences of multiple compositors. Apostrophes marking elision are rare, with only six occurrences (A2^v, A3^r, C1^v, C4^v, H3^v, and H4^r). There are only ten occurrences of 'hir'—one each on B2^r, C1^v, and C4^r, two on F1^r, and no fewer than five on H4^v—but 'her' is the dominant spelling throughout, with more than a hundred occurrences, including two on H4^v (both spellings occur in TLN 2266). Similarly, the form 'ile' (for 'I'll') is clearly dominant, with thirty occurrences, whereas 'Ile' is only used seven times (A3^v, A4^r, C1^v, E2^r, G1^v, G3^r, G4^r). The spellings 'lesse' and '-lesse' are preferred throughout, being used twenty-two times as against only one occurence of '-les': 'supperles' (B3^r, TLN 404). Accordingly, no easily discernible pattern of variant compositorial spellings seems to emerge.

Freeman has commented on the prominence of medial 'ou' in *Soliman and Perseda* in words such as 'bloud', 'gould' or 'honour' (including its derivative forms such as 'bloudy' or 'honourable').[73] There are nine occurrences of 'bloud' (A2^r, C2^r, C3^r (3×), F1^r, G4^v, H1^v, H2^r) as opposed to two of 'blood' (A4^r, B1^r); eight of 'gould' (B4^r, C3^r (2×), D3^r (2×), E1^r, E2^r, H1^r) as opposed to six of 'gold' (A3^v, A4^v, B1^r, B4^v, C4^v, D3^r) (note that both forms appear on D3^r); and sixteen of 'honour' (A3^v (2×), B3^v, B4^r, E1^r, E2^r, E2^v, E3^v (2×), E4^r (2×), F2^r (2×), F2^v, G1^r, I2^r) as opposed to thirteen of 'honor' (A3^v, A4^r (2×), B3^v, C1^r, C3^v (3×), D3^v, D4^v, E2^v, F2^v, H2^r) (note that both forms appear on A3^v, B3^v, E2^v, and F2^v).

Spellings are thus inconclusive in differentiating compositors. If two compositors set the text, the presence of the second might perhaps be suspected in sheet A, which has consistently '*Per.*' and never '*Perse.*', two of the six rare apostrophes, a clear preference for '-y[e]' over '-ie', no overrunning line that is optionally turned down, 'blood' and 'honor', as well as two of the six 'gold' spellings. However, 'bloudy' also occurs on A2^r, and 'honour' and 'honoured' on A3^v. All in all, the evidence does not point towards any firm conclusions: a single compositor may have set the entire text, or another compositor (or other compositors) may have set some of the text, perhaps sheet A, or part of sheet A, but conceivably also other parts of the text.

A notable feature of the printed text is the high incidence of type substitution. It is likely to have resulted variously from foul case, compositorial error, and type shortage. Most frequently type shortage affects italic capitals. Italics

---

[73] Freeman, 'The Printing of *The Spanish tragedy*', 198.

were used for proper names in speech headings and dialogue text, and since the supply of italic capitals seems to have been quite limited, roman capitals were sometimes substituted. This concerns chiefly letters that start prominent names and important initial words in stage directions, '*P*' ('*Perseda*', '*Piston*'), '*E*' ('*Erastus*', '*Enter*', '*Exit*'), and '*S*' ('*Soliman*'), as well as '*T*', of which few types seem to have been available. Similarly, '*VV*' was used when '*W*' was unavailable or in short supply. And a shortage of roman '*I*' seems to have led repeatedly to substitution by italic '*I*'.

Patterns of type substitution may yield information about how the typesetting proceeded (see Tables 1 to 6).

TABLE 1 WRONG-FOUNT P

P/P

	A	B	C	D	E	F	G	H	I
1ʳ		0/0	2/3	5/0	12/0	7/0	5/1	1/0	4+1*/0
1ᵛ		2/0	0/1	2/0	1/4	1/0	1/0	0/4	1/0
2ʳ	0/0	9/0	0/4	7/0	0/4	4/0	0/1	2/2	3/0
2ᵛ	3/0	15/1	0/0	4/2	0/0	1/0	8/0	12/0	0/0
3ʳ	7/0	8/0	1/0	5/0	0/0	2/0	9/3	7/1	
3ᵛ	3/0	1/1	0/0	3/0	0/0	7/0	1/6	5/0	
4ʳ	6/0	2/0	3/0	5/0	1/1	5/0	3/4	9/1	
4ᵛ	0/0	6/4	8/1	7/11	0/10	6/0	1/1	9+1*/0	
Total *P*	19/0	43/6	14/9	38/13	14/19	33/0	28/16	46/9	9/1
Outer forme	10/0	29/5	11/4	21/13	12/10	16/0	23/5	30/2	5/1
Inner forme	9/0	14/1	3/5	17/0	2/9	17/0	5/11	16/7	4/0

* substitution of italic for roman

TABLE 2 WRONG-FOUNT E

E/E

	A	B	C	D	E	F	G	H	I
1ʳ		0/0	7/0	10/0	4/0	6/0	5/0	4/0	3/0
1ᵛ		1/0	2/0	2/0	3/0	4/0	2/0	7/0	2/0
2ʳ	2/0	3/0	0/0	7/0	5/0	6/0	2/1	8/0	4/0
2ᵛ	4/0	0/0	0/0	8/0	3/0	8/0	1/0	2/0	2/0
3ʳ	4/0	1/0	3/0	6/0	4/0	4/0	7/0	1/0	
3ᵛ	5/0	5/0	1/0	4/0	0/7	0/0	8/0	2/0	
4ʳ	7/0	7/0	1/0	3/0	1/6	0/0	8/0	2/0	
4ᵛ	1/0	2/0	3/0	6/0	0/10	10/0	7/0	3/0	
Total *E*	23/0	19/0	17/0	46/0	20/23	38/0	40/1	29/0	11/0
Outer forme	9/0	3/0	13/0	30/0	11/10	28/0	20/0	10/0	5/0
Inner forme	14/0	16/0	4/0	16/0	9/13	10/0	20/1	19/0	6/0

Table 3 Wrong-fount S

S/S

	A	B	C	D	E	F	G	H	I
1r		1/0	1/0	0/0	0/0	1/0	3/0	3/0	5/0
1v		0/0	1/0	0/0	0/0	4/0	8/0	4/1	0/3
2r	0/0	0/0	2/0	0/0	0/0	3/0	0/0	4/0	1/2
2v	0/0	1/0	4/0	0/0	7/0	2/1	0/0	0/0	0/0
3r	0/0	3/0	3/0	1/0	7/0	7/1	2/0	5/0	
3v	0/0	2/0	1/0	0/0	6/0	9/0	3/0	3/0	
4r	0/0	0/0	0/0	0/0	7/0	1/6	4/0	7/2	
4v	2/0	0/0	0/0	0/0	1/0	0/5	6/0	0/8	
Total S	2/0	7/0	12/0	1/0	28/0	27/13	26/0	26/11	6/5
Outer forme	2/0	5/0	8/0	1/0	15/0	10/7	11/0	8/8	5/0
Inner forme	0/0	2/0	4/0	0/0	13/0	17/6	15/0	18/3	1/5

Table 4 Wrong-fount T

T/T

	A	B	C	D	E	F	G	H	I
1r		0/0	0/0	0/0	1/0	0/0	1/0	1/0	1/0
1v		1/0	0/0	0/0	0/0	2/0	1/0	2/0	2/1
2r	0/0	1/0	0/0	0/0	0/0	0/0	1/0	3/0	0/1
2v	0/0	4/0	2/0	0/0	0/0	0/0	2/0	0/0	0/0
3r	0/0	0/0	0/0	2/0	0/0	1/0	0/0	0/2	
3v	0/0	1/0	0/0	1/0	0/0	0/0	0/0	0/1	
4r	0/0	1/0	0/0	0/0	1/0	1/0	0/0	1/0	
4v	0/0	0/0	0/0	0/0	0/0	0/0	0/0	2/1	
Total T	0/0	8/0	2/0	3/0	2/0	4/0	5/0	9/4	3/2
Outer forme	0/0	4/0	2/0	2/0	1/0	1/0	3/0	3/3	1/0
Inner forme	0/0	4/0	0/0	1/0	1/0	3/0	2/0	6/1	2/2

Table 5 Wrong-fount I

I/*I*

	A	B	C	D	E	F	G	H	I
1[r]		10/0	17/0	10/0	10/1	9/1	8/1	6/0	6/0
1[v]		11/0	8/0	13/0	17/0	3/1	10/0	7/0	15/0
2[r]	6/0	14/0	4/2	9/0	11/0	12/1	11/0	7/0	8/1
2[v]	16/0	13/0	17/0	10/0	8/0	7/0	13/0	8/1	3/1
3[r]	12/0	9/0	12/0	6/0	5/0	7/0	13/0	10/0	
3[v]	7/0	3/1	9/1	8/0	6/0	4/0	8/0	11/0	
4[r]	2/0	10/0	4/0	19/4	13/0	7/0	7/0	7/0	
4[v]	15/0	3/0	10/0	9/4	12/0	15/3	8/4	8/9	
Total I	58/0	73/1	81/3	84/8	82/1	64/6	78/5	64/10	32/2
Outer forme	43/0	35/0	56/0	35/4	35/1	38/4	42/5	32/10	9/1
Inner forme	15/0	38/1	25/3	49/4	47/0	26/2	36/0	32/0	23/1

Table 6 W and VV

W / VV

	A	B	C	D	E	F	G	H	I
1[r]	0/0*	4/0	5/2	2/0	1/0	3/0	4/0	10/0	3/2
1[v]		3/0	4/0	6/0	3/0	6/0	4/0	4/2	2/0
2[r]	2/0*	2/0	9/2	4/4	3/0	2/0	1/0	0/5	4/6
2[v]	8/0	8/0	2/0	0/2	4/0	4/0	3/2	3/2	1/1
3[r]	3/0	4/0	3/0	2/0	4/0	2/0	1/4	2/4	
3[v]	0/0	5/0	3/0	5/0	1/0	6/0	4/0	1/3	
4[r]	4/0	3/0	7/0	3/1	2/0	4/0	2/2	2/3	
4[v]	10/0	6/2	7/1	1/1	3/0	2/0	6/1	1/2	
Total W / VV	27/0	35/2	40/5	23/8	21/0	29/0	25/9	23/21	10/9
Outer forme	21/0	22/2	17/3	5/3	12/0	11/0	14/7	16/8	4/3
Inner forme	6/0	13/0	23/2	18/5	9/0	18/0	11/2	7/13	6/6

* 'VV' occurs on A1[r] and 'W' on A2[r] in typefaces other than pica roman.

What the tables suggest is that setting was seriatim and not by formes. As has been pointed out, setting by formes 'can produce exclusive patterns of typographical usage that are isolated to just one forme of a sheet. The most common usage pattern consists of the substitution of letters in a second typeface for normal letters because of a shortage of the latter.'[74] In Q1 *Soliman and Perseda*, by contrast, patterns of substitution repeatedly continue from

[74] Adrian Weiss, 'Casting Compositors', p. 217.

the recto to the verso of the same leaf, thus including both formes. When setting sheet E, for instance, the compositor(s) ran out of italic E after E3^r and therefore had recourse to roman E on E3^v, E4^r, and E4^v.[75] In sheet F, after a last italic S was used at the head of F4^r (TLN 1622), the case seems to have been empty, leading to the substitution of eleven roman Ss on F4^r and F4^v. Similarly, in sheet H, after seven italic Ss had been set on H4^r, roman capitals had to substitute for the last two on that page and eight more on H4^v. When sheet C started being set, two italic Ps were available on C1^r, but when they had been set, roman P had to substitute for the next eight occurrences, three further down on C1^r, one on C1^v, and four on C2^r. (The case seems to have been replenished by the time C3^r was set.) The pattern of capital P in sheet G is somewhat less clear but may nonetheless be significant. From G1^r to G2^v, fourteen of sixteen Ps are in italics, but starting from G3^r, they seem to have been in short supply, leading to no fewer than fourteen substitutions from G3^r to G4^v.

It is worth pointing out that the text (or at least a significant part of it) seems to have been set seriatim despite the fact that setting by formes might have had advantages: given that almost the entire text is arranged as verse, casting off with accuracy would not have been difficult;[76] and given the shortage of type as evidenced by the many wrong-fount letters, setting by formes would have required fewer pages of type to stand simultaneously. On the other hand, seriatim setting may be unsurprising since *The Spanish Tragedy*, printed in the same printing house around the same time, was set in the same way.[77]

The series of wrong-fount T in sheets H and I (see Table 4) is not easy to explain. Only eleven italic Ts are tied up in sheet G and H1^r–2^r when three wrong-fount roman Ts were set in H3^{r-v}. Another three italic Ts were available for H4^{r-v}, and three more for I1^{r-v}, but one T each on H4^v, I1^v, and I2^r are again wrong-fount. On the one hand, it seems hard to believe that the case would have been depleted with only eleven italic Ts in use; on the other hand, the appearance of wrong-fount Ts from H3^r to H4^v and I1^v to I2^r can hardly be accidental and does suggest that the right fount was exhausted, given that no fewer than six roman Ts were set and that at no other point of the printing were more italic Ts needed. The explanation might be that the case was being

[75] That sheet E was not set by formes is corroborated by the misplaced line on E2^r (see above, pp. xviii–xix), an error that crosses inner and outer formes.

[76] Many speeches of Basilisco and Piston, though printed as if verse, lack verse rhythms and are probably mislined prose. The only short passages which are printed as prose are TLN 246–7 and 542–3.

[77] 'The pattern of wrong-fount employment demonstrates certainly that the setting was seriatim, and not by forme' (Freeman, 'The Printing of *The Spanish tragedy*', 189). Scepticism about the alleged frequency of setting by formes of Elizabethan play quartos was voiced as long ago as 1969 by D. F. McKenzie in his seminal essay, 'Printers of the Mind: Some Notes on Bibliographical Theories and Printing-House Practices', *Studies in Bibliography*, 22 (1969), 1–75, p. 38.

used concurrently for more than one printing job, but the sample is too small for the evidence to be conclusive.[78]

Type shortage may also account for certain uses of the form VV instead of W (see Table 6). On several occasions, the two forms seem to have been used continuously, Ws until they were exhausted, VVs until the W box was replenished. On B4^v, for instance, six Ws are followed by two VVs. At the beginning of C1^r, VV continues to be used (see TLN 518 and 519), although from TLN 527, Ws are again available. Similar patterns occur on C2^r, C4^v, and D2^{r-v}. In sheets H (from H2^v) and I (especially on I2^r), however, the two forms are alternated. Here, for instance, is the sequence on H2^v: VV, 3Ws, VV, W, VV; on H3^r: W, VV, W, 3VVs; and on I2^r: 2Ws, 3VVs, 2Ws, 3VVs. The different patterns of W / VV use in sheets B and C on the one hand and H and I on the other hand might at first suggest the presence of a second compositor who set the outer form of sheet H and the inner of half-sheet I. Yet the evidence for seriatim printing in sheet H is strong: the substitution of T for *T* on H3^r argues for fount depletion, which continues on H3^v (see Table 4), as does the substitution of S for *S* on H4^r, which continues on H4^v (see Table 3). It therefore seems more likely that the sole or chief compositor was inconsistent in dealing with type shortage: sometimes, a letter was used until it was exhausted, followed by substitution; sometimes, a depleted letter was used alternatingly with its substitute. Alternation is found for instance on B4^v with *P* / P where the order is: *P*, 2Ps, *P*, P, 4*P*s, P. Yet the same compositor who used *P* / P alternatingly set on the same page W until it was exhausted and then VV twice. Clearly, the compositor who set B4^v used both patterns, so there is no reason why he should not have set sheet H.

The massed appearance of VV and wrong-fount P, E, S, and T in several sheets suggests that the compositor(s) ran out of certain types.[79] The same is

---

[78] *Soliman and Perseda* was probably set from more than one type case, as is suggested by the fluctuating supply and demand for particular upper case italic sorts. As Freeman has commented, 'Wrong-fount analysis applied . . . to *Solyman and Perseda* . . . proves absolutely fruitless, possibly because the case was in use by more than one compositor for more than one book, possibly because some other text was distributed into it from time to time, or for any number of other reasons' (Freeman, 'The Printing of *The Spanish tragedy*', 188). For instance, wrong-fount S in sheet F may indicate that the inner and outer formes of sheet E were still standing when F4^r and F4^v were being set. If so, when the last remaining italic *S* had been set on F4^r (TLN 1622), fifty-five italic *S*s were in use, probably more than at any other point of the setting of the text. When H4^r was set, the supply of italic *S* was again low: the seven remaining types were set, after which roman S twice substituted for italic *S* (TLN 2226 and 2227), plus all of 'Soliman' was exceptionally in roman in TLN 2239. At this point, assuming all of sheet G was still standing, fifty-two italic *S*s were in use, not fifty-five, which means three *S*s appear to have been 'lost', perhaps due to a concurrent printing job.

[79] The reappearance of previously depleted letters suggests type was distributed after the setting of (1) the first lines of C1^r (as evidenced by W / VV substitution), (2) C2^r (W / WW substitution), (3) C4^v (W / VV substitution), (4) D2^v (*P* / P and W / VV substitution), (5) D4^v (*P* / P substitution); (6) E4^v (*E* / E substitution), (7) F4^v (*S* / S substitution), and (8) H4^v (*S* / S substitution). Given the occasional substitutions in situations where a case does not seem to have been empty, it appears difficult or impossible to say where else type was redistributed. For instance, on B2^v, TLN 335, a single instance of *P* / P substitution is followed by fifteen *P*s on the same page (starting at TLN 336), so it seems unlikely that the substitution was motivated

probably not true for roman I, even though like the letters examined above, it was frequently substituted. As Table 5 shows, a significant number of pages have one or two italic *I*s where roman I would be expected but where the reason is clearly not type shortage: B3^v, C2^r (2×), C3^v, E1^r, F1^r, F1^v, F2^r, G1^r, H2^v, I2^r. The reason may be 'resident fouling' of the kind well known from other printers' type-founts (including George Eld's roman I type-case in 1617).[80] It is true that wrong-fount italic *I*s tend to concentrate in late pages of a sheet— D4^r (4×), D4^v (4×), F4^v (3×), G4^v (4×), and H4^v (9×)—but in all these pages, roman Is appear alongside italic ones, suggesting that the compositor had not actually run out of roman I but that concentration in the typecase of italic *I* (which the compositor(s) perhaps tried to avoid in an unsystematic way) may have been increasing late in the setting of these sheets. All in all, patterns of letter substitutions in *Soliman and Perseda* thus allow only limited insight into the composition process, although they do provide evidence of seriatim setting rather than setting by formes.[81]

by fount depletion. Similarly, italic letters at the start of proper names are at times used alternatingly with their roman substitute, including on B4^v, G3^r and G4^r, just as W and VV are used alternatingly in sheets H and I. As a result, a full pattern of type distribution fails to emerge.

[80] Weiss, 'Casting Compositors', p. 219.
[81] Running titles have proved of little use in identifying patterns of imposition. No systematic type-identification has been undertaken for this edition. The method can only be confidently offered as evidence where the nature of the damage is sufficiently distinctive.

APPENDIX

The brackets contain suggested emendations with an indication of their earliest source. Problems and inconsistencies of italicization, capitalization, and punctuation have not been systematically recorded.

Abbreviations:

Q2: the second quarto, 1599
Hawkins: Thomas Hawkins, ed., *The Origin of the English Drama*, vol. 2, 1773
Smeeton: Joseph Smeeton, ed., *The Tragedie of Solimon and Perseda*, c.1805
Hazlitt: W. Carew Hazlitt, ed., *A Select Collection of Old English Plays*, vol. 5, 1874
Boas: F. S. Boas, ed., *The Works of Thomas Kyd*, 1901
Brereton: J. Le Gay Brereton, 'Notes on the Text of Kydd', *Englische Studien*, 37 (1907), 87–99
Murray: John J. Murray, ed., *The Tragedye of Solyman and Perseda*, 1991

Line number(s)

83	coustancie (constancie *Q2*)
115	hououred (honoured *Q2*)
120	bigbound (bigbon'd *Q2*)
121	Arthers (Archers *Q2*)
206	rhe (the *Q2*)
224	flint (faint *Brereton*)
228	Portinguze (Portinguize *Q2*)
229	golde, aboording (golde abounding *Boas*)[82]
246	arprooued (approoued *Q2*)
271	All (I, all *Boas*)
402	It it (It is *Q2*)
664	millious (millions *Q2*)
735	semblance (semblant *Hazlitt*)
743	ope (open *Hawkins*)
751	light (sight *Hazlitt*)
818	weakoning (weakling *Q2*)
821	shape (shaped *Hazlitt*)
967	pray (play *Boas*)
968	*Pistrn* (*Piston Q2*)
1075	*Philp.* (*Phil. Q2*)
1085	wiihall (withall *Q2*)
1176	about (a bout *Hawkins*)

[82] This emendation and the one at TLN 1617 were anticipated in manuscript annotations by Lewis Theobald ('gold-abounding'; 'Lines paralel') in the British Library copy C.34.b.45 of Q2. See Kahrl with Anderson, *The Garrick Collection*, p. 247.

1179	about (a bout *Hawkins*)
1180	(*final line on E2ᵛ Q2*)
1221–2	*the two lines are printed in inverted order (corrected in Q2)*
1221	ghost (ghoasts *Smeeton*; ghosts *Hazlitt*)
1226	he (be *Q2*)
1252	*before this line, a line is missing, misplaced at E2r, l. 1 (see above pp. xviii–xix)*
1254	onr (our *Q2*)
1290	pleasnre (pleasure *Q2*)
1323	this owne (this one *Hawkins*; his owne *Smeeton*)
1387	vnforrunate (vnfortunate *Q2*)
1388	aud (and *Q2*)
1437	strane (strand *Hawkins*)
1443	Citttzens (Cittizens *Q2*)
1493	herodian (Rhodian *Hawkins*)
1495	tougue (tongne *Q2*; tongue *Hawkins*)
1565	*Arias* (*Arrius Boas*; *Areus Murray*)
1584	lookes (lockes *Boas*)
1589	incombate (in combat *Hawkins*)
1617	Liues paralise (Lines parallel *Hawkins*)
1619	ar (at *Q2*)
1663	becaptiue (be captiue *Q2*)
1703	Reuies (Revives *Hawkins*)
1845	chalneged (chalenged *Q2*)
1955	morrow burning (marrow-burning *Hawkins*)[83]
2005	promisiug (promising *Q2*)
2010	a land (aland *Hawkins*)
2103	pinckanied (pinck-an-ey'd *Hawkins*; pinky-ey'd *Hazlitt*)
2146	Emperout (Emperour *Q2*)
2170	Troion (Trojan *Hawkins*)
2179	a dorned (adorned *Q2*)
2179	gifs (gifts *Q2*)
2183	Or (Are *Hawkins*)
2231	That if (That, if *Hawkins*)
2251	neare (nere *Q2*; ne'er *Hawkins*)
2260	thee, maintianing of *Persedas* (thee in maintaining P*ersedas Q2*; But <die> maintaining of *Persedas Boas*; But [fight] maintaining of *Persedas Murray*)
2309	heroyacall (heroical *Hawkins*)
2354	thy deaths (thy death *Hawkins*)
2382	witnesse (witnesses *Smeeton*)

[83] See footnote 82 above.

Line number

226	fought	*t* heavily smudged, may be italic; comma legible
463	laud	*l* imperfectly inked
671	*Amurath*	*u* imperfectly inked
1071	or	*o* barely visible, perhaps due to imperfect inking or damage
1140	teares	*t* imperfectly inked
1325+ c/w	E*rast.*	*a* tail not inked
1336	sit	final letter smudged and unclear
1434	little	²*t* only partly visible
1544	*E ast.*	second letter (*r*?), not printing
1709	to	*o* heavily stained
1766	prepare	*a* imperfectly inked, only partly visible
1837	Ile	*l* imperfectly inked, only partly visible
2101	little	*e* imperfectly inked, resembles *c*
2157	fortifie	*t* imperfectly inked, only partly visible
2214	*walles*	¹*l* imperfectly inked, its upper end invisible

Significant Differences Between Q1 (British Library Copy, Shelfmark c.34.b.44) and Q2 (Huntington Library Copy, Shelfmark 111499)

The most important difference between Q1 and Q2 is the removal of the misplaced line (TLN 1180) at the top of E2ʳ (see above, pp. xviii–xix) and its placement at the bottom of E2ᵛ. In order to keep the number of lines per page at thirty-seven, the compositor(s) of Q2 moved the line at the top of E2ᵛ in Q1 (TLN 1216) to the bottom of E2ʳ. Consequently, the catchword on E2ʳ also had to be changed, from 'Death.' in Q1 to 'To' in Q2.

LIST OF VARIANT READINGS

The preceding list of erroneous and doubtful readings contains many Q1 readings that Q2 emends. These variants are not repeated here.

Line number(s)	Q1	Q2
56	haue	hane[84]
79	how haue I	how I haue
145	serues	serue
200	with my	with a
252–3	For . . . table / To … conflicts.	For . . . mount. / I . . . conflicts
307	hayre	hayɹe

[84] The British Library copy of Q2 *Soliman and Perseda*, shelfmark 161.b.4, reads 'haue'.

389	run	ran
401	iustle	iust
411	no iron	iron
467	will I now	now will I
470	gould must	must golde
482	dossen	dossen of
506	crying	crying of
510	but	and
524	cryest	tryest
544	ye	you
554	the	the the
578	how	now
579	siege	siegd
647	speake	spake
682	Might	Wight
723	ouerthrowne	onerthrowne
741	*Fernando*	*Ferdinando*
741	lack	lɐck
746	thy	my
756	these	the
773	Heres	Heere is
776	Ladies	Ladie,
780	can	cau
780	coulours	colour
835	to	of
835	simple hart	heart
862	heauens	heanens
888	simplicitie	stmplicitie
904	remaines	remainer
910	mislead	misled
923	It	t
947	weares	wearɘs
952	By	Be
1035	sweete	deare
1053	this	the
1060	*Ferdinand*	*Ferdinando*
1093	a proclamation	proclamation
1095	paines	paine
1100	man	men
1110	*Perse.*	*Pist.*
1208	abridgde	abridge
1229	daughter	daughtet
1257	of armes	of arɯes
1327	Targets	Targers
1328	me thine	thee mine
1347	to	in

1356	*Ferdinandos*	*Ferdinados*
1409	one	each one
1410	you	yon
1456	thou	you
1490	eyes	eyet
1619	death	deate[85]
1661	Ianisaries	Ganisaries
1715	*Exeunt.*	*moved up one line*
1734	occasion	occasions
1981	*Witnesse*	*Witnesses.*
1997	worst	worse
2007	for to	to
2012	bewrayd	betraid
2019	accusations	accusation
2062	throw	thaow
2122	my	wy
2132	that	thet
2161	*Exeunt*	*Exennt*
2175	cup conquerour	cupcon querour
2183	enuious	euuious
2208	our teares	her teares
2231	ouermatch	ouer match
2232	liking shall	liking it shall
2263	with	wih
2267	ah what	all that
2272	didst not	didst thou not
2389	fortunes	fortune[86]

---

[85] The British Library copy of Q2 *Soliman and Perseda*, shelfmark 161.b.4, reads 'death'.
[86] Three overrunning lines in Q1 are set without overrun in Q2: sigs. TLN 486–7, 1087–8 and 2197–8. On one occasion, the overrun in Q2 occurs later (TLN 2310–11): 'vngratious | Counseller' (Q1); 'vngratious coun- | seller' (Q2).

THE

TRAGEDYE OF
SOLYMAN AND
PERSEDA.

VVherein is laide open, Loues
constancy, Fortunes incon-
stancy, and Deaths
Triumphs.

A T LONDON
Printed by *Edward Allde* for
Edward White, and are to be solde at
the little North doore of Paules
Church, at the signe of
the Gun.

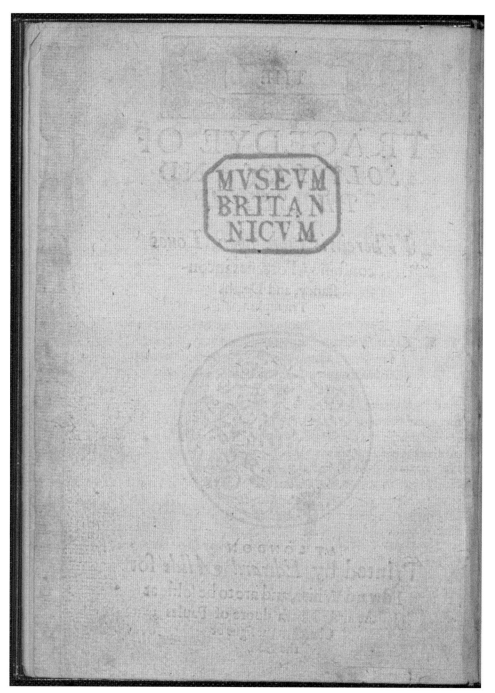

THE
Tragedie of *Soliman* and
Perseda.

Actus primus.

Enter Loue, Fortune, Death.

Loue.

WHat, *Death* and *Fortune* crosse the way of *Loue?*
For. Why, what is *Loue,* but *Fortunes* tenis-ball?
Death. Nay, what are you both, but subiects
    vnto *Death?*
And I commaund you to forbeare this place :
For heere the mouth of sad *Melpomene,*
Is wholy bent to tragedies discourse;
And what are Tragedies but acts of death?
Here meanes the wrathfull muse in seas of teares,
And lowd laments to tell a dismall tale :
A tale wherein she lately hath bestowed,
The huskie humour of her bloudy quill,
And now for tables takes her to her tung.
 Loue. Why thinkes *Death, Loue* knowes not the historie?
Of braue *Erastus* and his Rodian dame :
Twas I that made their harts consent to loue,
And therefore come I now as fittest person,
To serue for chorus to this Tragedie.
Had not I beene, they had not dyed so soone.
 Death. Had I not beene, they had not dyed so soone.

For. Nay then it seemes you both doo misse the marke,
Did not I change long loue to sudden hate?
And then rechange their hatred into loue:
And then from loue deliuer them to death?
Fortune is chorus. *Loue* and death be gone.

    Death. I tell thee *Fortune*, and thee wanton *Loue*,
I will not downe to euerlasting night,
Till I haue moralliz'd this Tragedy,
Whose cheefest actor was my sable dart.

    Loue. Nor will I vp into the brightsome sphere,
From whence I sprung, till in the chorus place,
I make it knowne to you and to the world,
What interest *Loue* hath in Tragedies.

    For. Nay then though *Fortune* haue delight in change,
Ile stay my flight, and cease to turne my wheelo,
Till I haue showne by demonstration,
What intrest I haue in a Tragedie.
Tush, *Fortune* can doo more then *Loue* or *Death*.

    Loue. Why stay we then, lets giue the Actors leaue,
And as occasion serues, make our returne.   *Exeunt.*

    Enter Erastus *and* Perseda.
    Erast. Why when *Perseda* wilt thou not assure me?
But shall I like a mastlesse ship at sea,
Goe euery way and not the way I would:
My loue hath lasted from mine infancie,
And still increased as I grew my selfe,
When did *Perseda* pastime in the streetes,
But her *Erastus* ouer-eied her sporte:
When didst thou with thy sampler in the Sunne,
Sit sowing with thy feres, but I was by
Marking thy lilly hands dexteritie:
Comparing it to twenty gratious things.
When didst thou sing a note that I could heare,
But I haue framde a dittie to the tune,
Figuring *Perseda* twenty kinde of waies.

    When

50

60

70

4

When didst thou goe to Church on hollidaies,
But I haue waited on thee too and fro :
Marking my times as Faulcons watch their flight.
When I haue mist thee how haue I lamented,
As if my thoughts had bene assured true.
Thus in my youth, now since I grew a man,
I haue perseuered to let thee know,
The meaning of my true hatts constancie:
Then be not nice *Perseda* as women woont,
To hasty louers whose fancy soone is fled:
My loue is of a long continuance,
And merites not a strangers recompence.

   Per. Enough *Erastus* thy *Perseda* knowes,
She whom thou wouldst haue thine, *Erastus* knowes,
   Erast. Nay my *Perseda* knowes, and then tis well.
   Per. I watch you vauntages, thine be it then,
I haue forgot the rest, but thats the effect:
Which to effect, accept this carkanet,
My Grandame on her death bed gaue it me,
And there, euen there I vow'd vnto my selfe,
To keepe the same vntill my wandring eye,
Should finde a harbour for my hart to dwell.
Euen in thy brest doo I elect my rest,
Let in my hart to keepe thine company.
   Erast. And sweet *Perseda* accept this ring,
To equall it, receiue my hart to boot,
It is no boot, for that was thine before?
And far more welcome is this change to me,
Then sunny daies to naked Sauages,
Or newes of pardon to a wretch condemde,
That waiteth for the fearefull stroke of death.
As carefull will I be to keepe this chaine,
As doth the mother keepe her children,
From water pits, or falling in the fire.
Ouer mine armour will I hang this chaine,
And when long combat makes my body faint,
The sight of this shall shew *Persedas* name.

A 3

And

And ad fresh courage to my fainting limmes.
This day the eger Turke of Tripolis,
The Knight of Malta, hououred for his worth,
And he thats titled by the golden spurre.
The Moore vpon his hot barbarian horse,
The fiery Spaniard bearing in his face,
The empresle of a noble warriour.
The sudden Frenchman, and the bigbound Dane,   120
And English Arthers hardy men at armes,
Eclipped Lyons of the westerne worlde:
Eche one of these approued combatants,
Aſſembled from seuerall corners of the world,
Are hither come to try their force in armes,
In honor of the Prince of Cipris nuptials.
Amongſt these worthies will *Eraſtus* troupe,
Though like a Gnat amongſt a hiue of Bees:
Know me by this thy pretious carkanet,
And if I thriue, in valour as the glaſſe   130
That takes the Sun-beames burning with his force:
Ile be the glaſſe, and thou that heauenly Sun,
From whence Ile borrow what I do atchieue.
And sweet *Perseda* vnnoted though I be,
Thy beauty yet shall make me knowne ere night.
     Per. Yong ſlippes are neuer graft in windy daies,
Yong ſchollers neuer entered with the rod,
Ah my *Eraſtus* there are Europes Knights,
That carry honour grauen in their helmes,
And they muſt winne it deere that winne it thence.   140
Let not my beauty prick thee to thy bane,
Better ſit ſtill then riſe and ouer-tane.
     Eraſt. Counſell me not, for my intent is ſworne,
And be my fortune as my loue deſerues.
     Per. So be thy fortune as thy features ſerues.
And then *Eraſtus* liues without compare.
          Enter a Meſſenger.
Here comes a Meſſenger to haſte me hence,
I know your meſſage, hath the Princeſſe ſent for me?
                              Meſſen.

6

Messen. She hath,and desires you to consort her to the
       Enter Piston .   (triumphes.
  Piston, Who saw my Master?
O sir,are you heeere?
The Prince and all the outlandish Gentlemen,
Are ready to goe to the triumphs,they stay for you.
   Erast. Goe sirra,bid my men bring my horse,
     and a dosen staues.
   *Pist.*You shall haue your horses and two dosen of staues.
               Exit Piston.
   Erast. Wish me good hap *Perseda* and Ile winne
Such glory,as no time shall ere race out,
Or end the period of my youth in blood.
   Per. Such fortune as the good *Andromache,*
Wisht valiant *Hector* wounded with the Greekes,
I wish *Erastus* in his maiden warres.
Orecome with valour these high minded Knights,
As with thy vertue thou hast conquered me,
Heauens heare my harty praier and it effect.   *Exeunt.*

   Enter Philippo,*the Prince of Cipris,* Basilisco,
     and all the Knights.
  Phil. Braue knights of Christendome,and turkish both,
Assembled heere in thirsty honors cause,
To be enrolled in the brasse leaued booke,
Of neuer wasting perpetuitie.
Put Lambe-like mildenes to your Lyons strength,
And be our tilting like two brothers sportes,
That exercise their war with friendly blowes.
Braue Prince of Cipris,and our sonne in law,
Welcome these worthies by their seuerall countries,
For in thy honor hither are they come,
To grace thy nuptials with their deeds at armes.
   Cipris. First welcome thrise renowned Englishman,
Graced by thy country,but ten times more
By thy approued valour in the field,
Vpon the onset of the enemy,

                       What

What is thy motto when thou spurres thy horse.

    Englishman. In Scotland was I made a Knight at armes,
Where for my countries cause I chargde my Launce:
In France I tooke the Standard from the King,
And giue the flower of Gallia in my crest.   190
Against the light foote Irish haue I serued,
And in my skinne beare tokens of their skenes:
Our word of courage all the world hath heard,
Saint George for England, and saint George for me.

    Cipris. Like welcome vnto thee faire Knight of **Fraunce**,
Well famed thou art for discipline in warre,
Vpon the incounter of thine enemy,
What is thy mot renowned Knight of Fraunce.

    French-man. In Italie I put my knighthoode on,   200
Where in my shirt but with my single Rapier,
I combated a Romane much renownd,
His weapons point impoysoned for my bane,
And yet my starres did bode my victory,
Saint Denis is for France and that for me.

    Cipris. Welcome *Castilian* too amongst the rest,
For fame doth sound thy valour with the rest:
Vpon thy first incounter of thy foe,
What is thy woord of courage braue man of Spaine?

    Spaniard. At fourteene yeeres of age was I made Knight,   210
When twenty thousand Spaniards were in field,
What time a daring Rutter made a challenge
To change a bullet with our swift flight shot,
And I with single heed and leuell hit,
The haughty challenger and strooke him dead.
The golden Fleece is that we cry vpon,
And Iaques, Iaques, is the Spaniards choice.

    Cipris. Next, welcome vnto thee renowned **Turke**,
Not for thy lay, but for thy worth in armes:
Vpon the first braue of thine enemy,
What is thy noted word of charge, braue Turke?   220

    Bruser. Against the Sophy in three pitched fields,
Vnder the conduct of great *Soliman*,

                                     Haue

Haue I bene chiefe commaunder of an hoaſt,
And put the flint heart Perſeans to the ſword.
The deſert plaines of Affricke haue I ſtaind,
With blood of Moores, and there in three ſet battels fought
Marcht conquerour through Aſia,
Along the coaſts held by the Portinguze,
Euen to the verge of golde, aboording Spaine
Hath *Bruſor* led a valiant troope of Turkes,
And made ſome Chriſtians kneele to *Mahomet*
Him we adore, and in his name I crie,
Mahomet for me and *Solyman.*

    Cip. Now Signeur *Baſiliſco* you we know,
And therefore giue not you a ſtrangers welcome,
You are a Rutter borne in Germanie,
Vpon the firſt encounter of your foe:
What is your braue vpon the enemy?

    Baſi. I fight not with my tongue, this is my Oratrix.
                 Laying his hand vpon his ſword.

    Cip. Why Signeur *Baſiliſco* is it a ſhe ſword?
    Baſi. I, and ſo are all blades with me: beholde my inſtance
Perdie, each female is the weaker veſſell,
And the vigour of this arme infringeth,
The temper of any blade, quoth my aſſertion,
And thereby gather, that this blade beeing arprooued wea-
  ker than this ſim, may very wel bear a feminine Epitheton.

    Cip. Tis well prooued, but whats the word that glories your
    Baſi. Sooth to ſay, the earth is my Countrey, (Countrey?
As the aire to the fowle, or the marine moiſture,
To the red guild fiſh: I repute my ſelfe no coward:
For humilitie ſhall mount. I keepe no table
To character my ſore-paſſed conflicts.
As I remember, there happened a ſore drought
In ſome part of Belgia, that the iucie graſſe,
Was ſeared with the Sunne Gods Element.
I held it pollicie, to put the men children
Of that climate to the ſword,
That the mothers teares might releeue the pearched earth.
              B   The

The men died,the women wept,and the graffe grew,
Els had my Frize-land horfe perifhed,
Whofe loffe would haue more grieued me,
Than the ruine of that whole Countrey.
Vpon a time in Ireland I fought,
On horfebacke with an hundred Kernes,
From *Titans* Eafterne vprife,to his Wefterne downe-fall:
Infomuch that my Steed began to faint:
I coniecturing the caufe to be want of water,difmounted:
In whichplace there was no fuch Element,
Enraged therefore with this Semitor,
All on foote like an Herculian offfpring,
Endured fome three or foure howers combat,
In which proceffe, my body diftilled fuch dewy fhowers of
That from the warlike wrinckles of my front,   (fwet,
My Palfray coold his thirft.
My mercy in conqueft, is equall with my manhood in fight,
The teare of an infant, hath bin the ranfome of a conquered
Whereby I purchafed the furname of *Pities adomant*. (cittie,
Rough wordes blowe my choller,
As the winde dooth Mulcibers worke houfe,
I haue no word,becaufe no countrey,
Each place is my habitation,
Therefore each countries word mine to pronounce.
Princes, what would you ?
I haue feene much,heard more, but done moft,
To be briefe,hee that will try me , let him waft mee with his
I am his,for fome fiue launces.   (arme.
Although it go againft my ftarres to ieft,
Yet to gratulate this beninge Prince,
I will fuppreffe my condition.
    Phylip. He is beholding to you greatly fir :
Mount ye braue Lordings,forwards to the tilt,
My felfe will cenfure of your chiualrie,
And with impartiall eyes behold your deedes,
Forward braue Ladies,place you to behold
The faire demeanor of thefe warlike Knights.   *Exeunt.*
                                                    Manet.

Manet Bafilifco.

Baf. I am melancholy: an humor of Venus belegereth me.
I haue reiected with contemptable frownes,
The fweet glances of many amorous girles, or rather ladies:
But certes, I am now captiuated with the reflecting eye
Of that admirable comet *Perfeda.*
I will place her to behold my triumphes,
And do woonders in hir fight,
O heauens, fhe comes, accompanied with a child,
Whofe chin beares no impreffion of manhood,
Not an hayre, not an excrement.

Enter Eraftus, Perfeda, *and* Pyftan.

Eraft. My fweet *Perfeda.*

Exeunt Eraftus *and* Perfeda.

Baf. Peace Infant thou blafphemeft.
Pift. You are deceiued fir, he fwore not,
Baf. I tell thee Iefter he did worfe, he cald that Ladie his,
Pift. Iefter: *O extempore, o flores!*
Baf. O harfh vnedicate, illiterate pefant,
Thou abufeft the phrafe of the Latine.
Pift. By gods filh friend, take you the Latins part, ile abufe
Baf. What faunce dread of our indignation?　　(you to.
Pift. Saunce : what languidge is that?
I thinke thou art a worde maker by thine occupation.
Baf. I, tearmeft thou me of an occupation,
Nay then this fierie humor of choller is fuppreft,
By the thought of loue. Faire Ladie,
Pift. Now by my troth fhe is gon.
Baf. I, hath the Infant tranfported her hence,
He faw my anger figured in my brow,
And at his beft aduantage ftole away,
But I will follow for reuenge.
Pift. Naye, but here you fir,
I muft talke with you before you goe.

Then Pifton *gets on his back, and puls him downe.*
Baf. O if thou beeft magnanimious, come before me.
Pift. Naye, if thou beeft a right warrior, get fró vnder me.

B 2　　　　　　　*Baf.*

II

Baſ. What wouldſt thou haue me a *Typhon,*
To beare vp *Peleon or Oſſa?*

   Piſt. Typhon me no *Typhons,*
But ſweare vpon my Dudgin dagger,
Not to go till I giue thee leaue,
But ſtay with me, and looke vpon the tilters.

    Baſ. O thou ſeekſt thereby to dim my glory.

    Piſt. I care not for that, wilt thou not ſweare?

    Baſ. O I ſweare, I ſweare.

               He ſweareth him on his Dagger.

    Piſt. By the contents of this blade,

    Baſ. By the contents of this blade.

    Piſt. I the aforeſaid *Baſiliſco,*

    Baſ. I the aforeſaid *Baſiliſco,*
Knight good fellow, knight, knight.

    Piſt. Knaue good fellow, knaue, knaue.
Will not offer to go from the ſide of *Piſton.*

    Baſ. Will not offer to go from the ſide of *Pyſton,*

    Piſt. Without the leaue of the ſaid *Piſton* obtained,

    Baſ. Without the leaue of the ſaid *Piſton,*
Licenſed, obtayned and granted.

    Piſt. Inioy thy life and liue, I giue it thee.

    Baſ. I inioy my life at thy hands, I confeſſe it,
I am vp, but that I am religious in mine oath.

    Piſt. What would you do ſir, what would you do,
Will you vp the ladder ſir, and ſee the tilting.

         Then they go vp the ladders, and they ſound
                   within to the firſt courſe.

    Baſ. Better a Dog fawne on me, then barke,

    Piſt. Now ſir, how likes thou this courſe.

    Baſ. Their Launces were coucht to hie,
And their Steedes ill borne.

    Piſt. It may be ſo, it may be ſo,
              Sound to the ſecond courſe.
Now ſir, how like you this courſe.

    Baſ. Prettie, prettie, but not famous,
Well for a learner, but not for a warriour.

                                     Piſt.

340

350

360

370

Pist. By my faith, me thought it was excellent.

Baf. I in the eye of an infant, a Peacocks taile is glorious.

Sound to the third course.

Pist. O well run, the baye horffe with the blew taile,

And the filuer knight, are both downe,

By Cocke and Pie, and Moufe foote,

The Englifh man is a fine Knight.

Baf. Now by the marble face of the Welkin,

Hee is a braue warriour.

Pist. What an oath is there, fie vpon thee extortioner.

Baf. Now comes in the infant that courts my miftreffe,

Sound to the fourth course.

Oh that my launce were in my reft,

And my Beauer clofd for this encounter.

Pist. O well ran, my maifter hath ouerthrown the Turke.

Baf. Now fie vpon the Turke,

To be difmounted by a Childe it vexeth me.

Sound to the fift course.   "(man.

Pist. O wel run Maifter, he hath ouerthrown the French-

Baf. It is the fury of his horfe, not the ftrength of his arme

I would thou wouldft remit my oath,

That I might affaile thy maifter.

Pist. I giue thee leaue, go to thy deftruction,

But fyrra wheres thy horfe?

Baf. Why my Page ftands holding him by the bridle.

Pist. Well goe mount thee, goe.

Baf. I go, and *Fortune* guide my Launce.

Exit Bafilifco.

Pist. Take the braginft knaue in chriftendom with thee:

Trulie I am forrie for him,

He iuft like a knight, heele iuftle like a Iade,

It it a world to heere the foole prate and brag,

He will iet as if it were a Goofe on a greene:

He goes many times fupperles to bed,

And yet he takes Phifick to make him leane.

Laft night he was bidden to a Gentlewomans to fupper,

And becaufe he would not be put to carue,

B 3   He

He wore his hand in a scarfe, and said he was wounded:
He weares a coloured lath in his scabberd,
And when twas found vpon him, he said he was wrathfull,   410
He might not weare no iron. He weres Ciuet,
And when it was askt him, where he had that muske,
He said, all his kindred smelt so:
Is not this a counterfet foole?
Well ile vp and see how he speedes.

                              Sound the sixt course,
Now by the faith of a squire, he is a very faint knight,
Why my maister hath ouerthrowne him
And his Curtall, both to the ground,   420
I shall haue olde laughing,
It will be better then the Fox in the hole for me.

          Sound: Enter Phylippo, Erastus, Ferdinando,
                    Lucina, *and all the Knights.*
    Cypr. Braue Gentlemen, by all your free consents,
This Knight vnknowne, hath best demeand himselfe,
According to the proclimation made,
The prize and honor of the day is his,
But now vnmaske thy selfe, that we may see,
What warlike wrinckles time hath charactered,   430
With ages print vpon thy warlike face.
    English. Accord to his request, braue man at armes,
And let me see the face that vanquished me.
    French. Vnmaske thy selfe, thou well approoued knight.
    Turke. I long to see thy face braue warriour.
    Luci. Nay valiant sir, we may not be denide,
Faire Ladies should be coye to showe their faces,
Least that the sun should tan them with his beames,
Ile be your page this once, for to disarme you.
    Pist. Thats the reason, that he shall helpe   440
Your husband to arme his head,
Oh the pollicie of this age is wonderfull.
    Phyllyp. What young *Erastus,* is it possible?
    Cipr. Erastus be thou honoured for this deed.
    English. So yong, and of such good accomplishment,
                                            Thriue

Thriue faire beginner as this time doth promise,
In vertue, valour, and all worthinesse :
Giue me thy hand, I vowe my selfe thy friend.

Erast. Thanks worthie sir, whose fauourable hand,
Hath entred such a youngling in the warre,
And thanks vnto you all, braue worthy sirs,
Impose me taske, how I may do you good,
Erastus will be dutifull in all.

Phyl. Leaue protestations now, and let vs hie,
To tread lauolto, that is womens walke,
There spend we the remainder of the day.

           Exeunt. Manet Ferdinando.

Ferdi. Though ouerborne, and foyled in my course,
Yet haue I partners in mine infamie.
Tis wondrous, that so yong a toward warriour,
Should bide the shock of such approoued knights,
As he this day hath matcht and mated too,
But vertue should not enuie good desert,
Therefore *Erastus* happy, laud thy fortune,
But my *Lucina*, how she changed her couler,
When at the encounter I did loose a stirrop,
Hanging her head as partner of my shame,
Therefore will I now goe visit her,
And please her with this Carcanet of worth,
Which by good fortune I haue found to day,
When valour failes, then gould must make the way.   *Exit.*

      Enter Basilisco *riding of a Mule.*

Bas. O cursed *Fortune* enemy to *Fame*,
Thus to disgrace thy honoured name,
By ouerthrowing him that far hath spred thy praise,
Beyond the course of *Titans* burning raies,

              Enter Piston.

Page set aside the iesture of my enemie,
Giue him a Fidlers fee, and send him packing.

Pist. Ho, God saue you sir, haue you burst your shin,
 Bas. I villaine, I haue broke my shin bone,
My back bone, my channell bone, and my thigh bone,

                      Be-

Beside two doſſen ſmall inferior bones,

Piſt. A ſhrewd loſſe by my faith ſir,
But wheres your courſers taile.

Baſ. He loſt the ſame in ſeruice.

Piſt. There was a hot piece of ſeruice, where he loſt his
But how chance his noſe is ſlit.   (taile

Baſ. For preſumption, for couering the Emperors Mare.

Piſt. Marrie a foule fault, but why are his eares cut?

Baſ. For neighing in the Emperours Court.

Piſt. Why then thy Horſe hath bin a Colt in his time,

Baſ. True, thou haſt ſaid.
O touch not the cheeke of my Palphrey,
Leaſt he diſmount me while my wounds are greene,
Page, run, bid the ſurgion bring his inciſion.
Yet ſtay ile ride along with thee my ſelfe.   *Exit.*

Piſt. And ile beare you companie,

> Piſton *getteth vp on his Aſſe, and rideth with him*
> *to the doore, and meeteth the Cryer.*

Enter the Cryer.

Piſt. Come ſirra, let me ſee how finely youle cry this chaine

Cryer. Why what was it worth?   (worth,

Piſt. It was woorth more, then thou and all thy kin are

Cryer. It may be ſo, but what muſt he haue that findes it?

Piſt. Why a hundred Crownes.

Cryer. Why then ile haue ten for the crying it.

Piſt. Ten Crownes, and had but ſix pence,
For crying a little wench of thirty yeares old & vpwards,
That had loſt her ſelfe betwixt a tauerne & a bawdie houſe.

Cryer. I that was a wench, but this is Golde,
Shee was poore, but this is rich.

Piſt. Why then by this reckoning, a Hackney man
Should haue ten ſhillings for horſing a Gentlewoman,
Where he hath but ten pence of a begger.

Cryer. VVhy and reaſon good,
Let them paie, that beſt may,
As the Lawyers vſe their rich Clyents,

VVhen

16

VVhen they let the poore go vnder *Forma pauperis.*

 Pift. VVhy then I pray thee crie the Chaine for me,

   Sub forma pauperis,

For money goes very low with me at this time.

 Cryer. I fir, but your maifter is, though you be not.

 Pift. I but hee muft not know

That thou cryeft the Chaine for me,

I do but vfe thee to faue me a labour,

That am to make inquirie after it,

 Cry. Well fir, youle fee me confidered, will you not ?

 Pift. I marry will I, why what lighter paiment can there

   be, then confideration.

Cryer. O yes.

    Enter Eraftus.

 Eraftus. How now firra, what are you crying?

 Cryer. A chaine fir, a chaine, that your man bad me crie.

 Eraftus. Get you away firra, I aduife you

Meddle with no Chaines of mine,   *Exit* Cryer.

You paltrie knaue, how durft thou be fo bould,

To crie the chaine, when I bid thou fhouldft not,

Did I not bid thee onely vnderhand,

Make priuie inquirie for it through the towne,

Leaft publike rumor might aduertife her,

Whofe knowledge were to me a fecond death?

 Pift. Why would you haue me runne vp and downe the

   towne ? and my fhooes are doone.

 Eraft. What you want in fhooes, ile giue ye in blowes.

 Pift. I pray you fir hold your hands,

And as I am an honeft man,

Ile do the beft I can to finde your chaine. *Exit* Pifton.

 Eraft. Ah treacherous *Fortune,* enemy to *Loue,*

Didft thou aduaunce me for my greater fall,

In dalying war, I loft my chiefeft peace,

In hunting after praife, I loft my loue,

And in loues fhipwrack will my life mifcarrie,

Take thou the honor, and giue me the chaine,

Wherein was linkt the fum of my delight.

    C   VVhen

When she deliuered me the Carkanet,
Keepe it quoth she, as thou wouldst keepe my selfe:
I kept it not, and therefore she is lost,
And lost with hir is all my happinesse,
And losse of happines is worse then death.
Come therefore gentle death and ease my griefe,
Cut short what malice *Fortune* misintends,
But stay a while good *Death*, and let me liue,
Time may restore what *Fortune* tooke from me :
Ah no, great losses sildome are restord.
What if my Chaine shall neuer be restord,
My innocence shall cleare my negligence.
Ah! but my loue is cerimonious,
And lookes for iustice at her louers hand,
Within forst furrowes of her clowding brow,
As stormes that fall amid a sun shine day,
I read her iust desires, and my decay.   *Exit.*

Enter Solyman, Haleb, Amarath, *and*
Ianesaries.
Soly. I long till *Brusor* be returnd from *Rhodes*,
To know how he hath borne him gainst the Christians,
That are assembled there to trie their valour,
But more to be well assured by him,
How *Rhodes* is fenc'd, and how I best may lay,
My neuer failing siege to win that plot,
For by the holy Alcaron I sweare,
Ile call my Souldiers home from *Persia*,
And let the Sophie breath, and from the *Russian* broiles
Call home my hardie, dauntlesse Ianisaries,
And from the other skirts of Christendome,
Call home my Bassowes and my men of war,
And so beleager *Rhodes* by sea and land.
That Key will serue to open all the gates,
Through which our passage cannot finde a stop,
Till it haue prickt the hart of Christendome,
Which now that paltrie Iland keepes from scath.

Say

Say brother *Amurath*, and *Haleb*, say,
What thinke you of our resolution?

    Amura. Great *Soliman*, heauens onely substitute,
And earths commander vnder Mahomet :
So counsell I, as thou thy selfe hast said.

    Haleb. Pardon me dread Soueraigne, *I* hold it not
Good pollicie, to call your forces home
From *Persea* and *Polonia*, bending them
Vpon a paltrie *Ile* of small defence.
A common presse of base superfluous Turkes,
May soone be leuied for so slight a taske.
Ah *Soliman*, whose name hath shakt thy foes,
As withered leaues with Autume throwen downe,
Fog not thy glory with so fowle eclipse,
Let not thy Souldiers sound a base retire,
Till *Persea* stoope, and thou be conquerour.
What scandall were it to thy mightinesse,
After so many valiant Bassowes slaine,
Whose bloud hath bin manured to their earth,
Whose bones hath made their deepe waies passable.
To sound a homeward, dull, and harsh retreate,
Without a conquest, or a meane reuenge,
Striue not for *Rhodes*, by letting *Persea* slip,
The ones a Lyon almost brought to death,
Whose skin will counteruaile the hunters toile ;
The other is a Waspe with threatning sting.
Whose Hunny is not worth the taking vp.

    Amu. Why *Haleb* didst thou not heare our brother sweare
Vpon the Alcaron religiously :
That he would make an vniuersall Campe
Of all his scattered legions : and darest thou
Infer a reason why it is not meete,
After his Highnes sweares it shall be so,
VVere it not thou art my fathers sonne,
And striuing kindnes wrestled not with ire,
I would not hence, till I had let thee know,
VVhat twere to thwart a Monarchs holy oath.

                C 2   *Haleb.*

*Haleb.*Why,his highnes gaue me leaue to speake my wil,
And far from flattery I spoke my minde,
And did discharge a faithfull subiects loue,   630
Thou *Aristippus* like didst flatter him,
Not like my brother,or a man of worth,
And for his highnesse vowe I crost it not,
But gaue my censure,as his highnesse bad,
Now for thy chastisment,know *Amurath*,
I scorne them as a rechlesse Lion scornes,
The humming of a gnat in Summers night,

    Amur. I take it *Haleb* thou art friend to Rhodes.
    Haleb. Not halfe so much am I a friend to Rhodes,
As thou art enemy to thy Soueraigne.   640
    Amur. I charge thee say wherein,or else by Mahomet,
Ile hazard dutie in my Soueraignes presence.
    *Haleb.*Not for thy threats,but for my selfe I say,
It is not meete, that one so base as thou,
Shouldst come about the person of a King,
    Soli. Must I giue aime to this presumption?
    *Amur.*Your Highnesse knowes,I speake in dutious loue.
    Haleb. Your Highnes knowes I spake at your command,
And to the purpose, far from flattery.
    Amu. Thinks thou I flatter,now I flatter not,   650
           Then he kils Haleb.
    Soli. What dismall Planets guides this fatall hower,
Villaine, thy brothers grones do call for thee.
           Then Soliman *kils* Amurath.
To wander with them through eternall night.
    Amu. Oh *Soliman* for louing thee I die,
    Soli. No *Amurath*, for murthering him thou dyest:
Oh *Haleb* how shall I begin to mourne,
Or how shall I begin to shed salt teares.
For whom no wordes nor teares can well suffice.   660
Ah that my rich imperiall Diadem,
Could satiffie thy cruell destinie:
Or that a thousand of our Turkish soules,
Or twenty thousand millious of our foes,

                    Could

Coul'd ranfome thee from fell deaths tirannie,
To win thy life. would *Soliman* be poore,
And liue in feruile bondage all my dayes,
Accurfed *Amurath*, that for a worthleffe caufe,
In bloud hath fhortned our fweet *Halebs* dayes,
Ah what is dearer bond then brotherhood,
Yet *Amurath* thou wert my brother too,
If wilfull folly did not blind mine eyes,
I, I, and thou as vertuous as *Haleb*,
And I as deare to thee as vnto *Haleb*,
And thou as neere to me as *Haleb* was,
Ah *Amurath* : why wert thou fo vnkind to him
For vttering but a thwarting word?
And *Haleb*, why did not thy harts counfell,
Bridle the fond intemperance of thy tongue?
Nay wretched *Solyman*, why didſt not thou
Withhould thy hand, from heaping bloud on bloud,
Might I not better fpare one ioy then both,
If loue of *Haleb* forſt me on to wrath,
Curſt be that wrath that is the way to death,
If iuſtice forſt me on, curſt be that iuſtice
That makes the brother, Butcher of his brother,
Come Ianiſaries, and helpe me to lament,
And beare my ioyes on either fide of me:
I, late my ioyes, but now my lafting forrow,
Thus, thus, let *Soliman* paffe on his way,
Bearing in either hand his hearts decay.　*Exeunt.*

Enter Chorus.

Loue. Now *Death* and *Fortune* which of all vs three,
Hath in the Actors fhowne the greateſt power.
Haue not I taught *Eraſtus* and *Perſeda*,
By mutuall tokens to feale vp their loues?
　Fortune. I but thofe tokens, the Ring and Carkanet,
Were *Fortunes* gifts, *Loue* giues no gould or iewels.
　Loue. Why what is iewels, or what is gould but earth,
An humor knit together by compreffion,

C 3　　　　　　　　And

And by the worlds bright eye, first brought to light,
Onely to feed mens eyes with vaine delight.
Loues workes are more then of a mortall temper,
I couple minds together by consent.
Who gaue Rhodes Princes to the Ciprian Prince: but *Loue.*

For. Fortune that first by chance brought them together,
For till by *Fortune* persons meete each other,
Thou canst not teach their eyes to wound their hearts.

Loue. I made those Knights of seuerall sect and countries
Each one by armes to honor his beloued,

For. Nay one alone to honor his beloued,
The rest by turning of my tickle wheele,
Came short in reaching of faire honors marke:
I gaue *Erastus* onely that dayes prize,
A sweete renowne, but mixt with bitter sorrow:
For in conclusion of his happines,
I made him loose the pretious Carcanet,
Whereon depended all his hope and ioy.

Death. And more then so: for he that found the chaine,
Euen for that Chaine shall be depriued of life.

Loue. Besides, *Loue* hath inforst a foole,
The fond Bragardo to presume to armes.

For. I but thou seest how he was ouerthrowne,
By *Fortunes* high displeasure.

Death. I and by *Death* had beene surprisd,
If Fates had giuen me leaue:
But what I mist in him and in the rest,
I did accomplish on *Haleb* and *Amurath,*
The worthie brethren of great *Soliman,*
But wherefore stay we, let the sequele prooue,
Who is greatest, *Fortune, Death,* or *Loue.*   *Exeunt.*

Enter Ferdinando *and* Lucina.

Fer. As fits the time, so now well fits the place,
To coole affection with our woords and lookes.
If in our thoughts be semblance simpathic.

Luci. My words, my lookes, my thoughts are all on thee.
                                        Fer-

710

720

730

Ferdinando is *Lucinaes* onely ioy.

   Ferdi. What pledge thereof?

   Luci. An oath, a hand, a kisse.

   Ferdi. O holy oath, faire hand, and sugred kisse :
Oh neuer may *Fernando* lack such blisse.
But say my deare, when shall the gates of heauen ?
Stand all wide ope for celestiall Gods,
With gladsome lookes to gase at *Hymens* robes.
When shall the graces, or *Lucinas* hand,
With Rosie chaplets deck thy golden tresses,
And *Cupid* bring me to thy nuptiall bed,
Where thou in ioy and pleasure must attend.
A blissfull war with me thy chiefest friend.

   Lucina. Full fraught with loue, and burning with desire,
I long haue longd for light of *Hymens* lights.

   Ferdi. Then that same day, whose warme & pleasant sight,
Brings in the spring, with many gladsome flowers,
Be our first day of ioy and perfect peace:
Till when, receiue this pretious Carcanet,
In signe, that as these linkes are interlaced,
So both our hearts are still combind in one,
Which neuer can be parted but by death.

       Enter Basilisco *and* Perseda.

   Luci. And if I liue this shall not be forgot :
But see *Ferdinando* where *Perseda* comes,
Whom women loue for vertue, men for bewty,
All the world loues, none hates but enuie.

   Bas. All haile braue Cauelere : God morrow Madam,
The fairest shine that shall this day be seene.
Except *Persedas* beautious excelence,
Shame to loues Queene, and Empresse of my thoughts.

   Ferdi. Marry thrise happy is *Persedas* chance,
To haue so braue a champion to hir Squire.

   Bas. Hir Squire : her Knight, and who so else denies,
Shall feele the rigour of my Sword and Launce.

   Ferdi. O Sir, not I.

   Luci. Heres none but friends, yet let me chalengeyou,

                          For

For gracing me with a malignant ftile,
That I was faireft, and yet *Perſeda* fayrer.
We Ladies ſtand vpon our beauties much.

 Perſe. Herein *Lucina* let me buckler him.
 Baſ. Not Mars himſelfe had eare ſo faire a Buckler.
 Perſe. Loue makes him blinde,
And blind can iudge no coulours.
 Luci. Why then the mends is made, and we ſtill friends, 780
 Perſe. Still friends, ſtill foes, ſhe weares my Carcanet,
Ah falſe *Eraſtus*, how am I betraid.
 Luci. What ailes you madam, that your coulor changes.
 Perſe. A ſuddaine qualme, I therefore take my leaue.
 Luci. Weele bring you home,
 Perſe. No, I ſhall ſoone get home.
 Luci. Why then farewell: *Fernando* lets away.
       Exeunt Ferdinando *and* Lucina.
 Baſ. Say worlds bright ſtarre,   790
Whence ſprings this ſuddaine change,
Is it vnkindnes at the little praiſe
I gaue *Lucina* with my gloſing ſtile?
 Perſe. No, no, her beautie far ſurpaſſeth mine,
And from my neck, her neck hath woone the praiſe.
 Baſ. What is it then, if loue of this my perſon,
By fauour and by iuſtice of the heauens,
At laſt haue percſt through thy tralucent breſt,
And thou miſdoubts, perhaps that ile proue coye, 800
Oh be aſſur'd tis far from noble thoughts,
To tyranniſe ouer a yeelding foe.
Therefore be blithe, ſweete loue abandon feare,
I will forget thy former crueltie.
 Perſe. Ah falſe *Eraſtus* full of treachrie.
 Baſ. I alwaies told you that ſuch coward knights,
VVere faithleſſe ſwaines and worthie no reſpect,
But tell me ſweete loue, what is his offence?
That I with words and ſtripes may chaſtice him,
And bring him bound for thee to tread vpon.
 Perſe. Now muſt I find the meanes to rid him hence, 810
              Go

Go thou foorthwith arme thee from top to toe,
And come an houre hence vnto my lodging,
Then will I tell thee this offence at large,
And thou in my behalfe shalt worke reuenge.

Baf. I thus should men of valour be imployd,
This is good argument of thy trueloue,
I go, make reconing that *Erastus* dyes,
Vnlesse forewarnd, the weakoning coward flies,
       Exit Basilisco.

Per. Thou foolish coward flies. *Erastus* liues,
The fayrest shape, but fowlest minded man,
That ere sunne saw within our hemyspheare,
My tongue to tell my woes is all to weake,
I must vnclaspe me, or my heart will breake:
But inward cares are most pent in with greefe,
Vnclasping therefore yeeldes me no releefe.
Ah that my moyst and cloud compacted braine,
Could spend my cares in showers of weeping raine.
But scalding sighes like blasts of boysterous windes,
Hinder my teares from falling on the ground,
And I must die by closure of my wound.
Ah false *Erastus*, how had I misdoone,
That thou shouldst quit my loue with such a scorne.
     !*Enter* Erastus.
Herecomes the Synon to my simple hart,
Ile frame my selfe to his dissembling art.

Eraft. Desire perswades me on, feare puls me backe:
Tush I will to her, innocence is bould,
How fares *Perseda* my sweete second selfe?

Perfe. Well, now *Erastus* my hearts onely ioy
Is come to ioyne both hearts in vnion.

Eraft. And till I came whereas my loue did dwell,
My pleasure was but paine, my solace woe.

Per. What loue meanes my *Erastus*, pray thee tell?

Eraft. Matchlesse *Perseda*, she that gaue me strength,
To win late conquest from many victors hands,
Thy name was conquerour, not my chiualrie:
       D   Thy

Thy lookes did arme me, not my coate of steele,
Thy beautie did defend me, not my force.
Thy fauours bore me, not my light foote Steed,   850
Therefore to thee I owe both loue and life.
But wherefore makes *Perseda* such a doubt,
As if *Erastus* could forget himselfe:
Which if I do, all vengeance light on me.

 Perse. Aye me, how gracelesse are these wicked men?
I can no longer hould my patience.
Ah how thine eyes can forge alluring lookes,
And faine deepe oathes to wound poore sillie maides,
Are there no honest drops in all thy cheekes,
To check thy fraudfull countenance with a blush: 860
Calst thou me loue, and louest another better,
If heauens were iust, thy teeth would teare thy tongue,
For this thy periurde false disloialtie.
If heauens were iust, men should haue open brests,
That we therein might read their guilefull thoughts.
If heauens were iust, that power that forceth loue,
Would neuer couple Wooltes and Lambes together.
Yes, heauens are iust, but thou art so corrupt,
That in thee, all their influence dooth change,   870
As in the Spider good things turne to poyson.
Ah false *Erastus*, how had I misdone?
That thou shouldst pawne my true affections pledge,
To her whose worth will neuer equall mine.
What, is *Lucinaes* wealth exceeding mine?
Yet mine sufficient to encounter thine.
Is she more faire then I? thats not my fault,
Nor her desart? whats beauty but a blast?
Soone cropt with age, or with infirmities.
Is she more wise? her yeares are more then mine.   880
What ere she be? my loue was more then hers,
And for her chastitie let others iudge.
But what talke I of her? the fault is thine,
If I were so disgratious in thine eye,
That she must needes inioy my interest,

Why

Why didst thou deck her with my ornament?
Could nothing serue her but the Carcanet?
Which as my life I gaue to thee in charge,
Couldst thou abuse my true simplicitie?
Whose greatest fault was ouer louing thee,
Ile keepe no tokens of thy periury.
Heere giue her this, *Perseda* now is free,
And all my former loue is turnd to hate.

    Erast. Ah stay my sweete *Perseda* heare me speake.
    Perse. What are thy words? but Syrens guilefull songs:
That please the eare, but seeke to spoile the heart.
    Erast. Then view my teares, that plead for innocence,
    Perse. VVhat are thy teares? but *Circes* magike seas,
VVhere none scape wrackt, but blindfould Marriners.
    Erast. If words & teares displease, then view my lookes,
That plead for mercy at thy rigorous hands.
    Perse. VVhat are thy lookes? but like the Cockatrice,
That seekes to wound poore silly passengers.
    Erast. If words, nor teares, nor lookes, may win remorse,
VVhat then remaines for my perplexed heart?
Hath no interpreters but words, or teares, or lookes.
    Perse. And they are all as false as thou thy selfe.
                   Exit Perseda.
    Erast. Hard doome of death before my case be knowne,
My iudge vniust, and yet I cannot blame her,
Since Loue and iealousie mislead her thus.
My selfe in fault, and yet not worthie blame,
Because that Fortune made the fault, not Loue.
The ground of her vnkindnes growes, because I lost
The pretious Carcanet she gaue to me:
Lucina hath it, as her words import,
But how she got it, heauens knowes, not I,
Yet this is some aleagement to my sorrow,
That if I can but get the Chaine againe,
I bouldly then shall let *Perseda* know,
That she hath wrongd *Erastus* and her frend:
Ah Loue, and if thou beest of heauenly power,

                  D 2   Inspire

Inspire me with some present stratagem,
It must be so, *Lucinas* a franke Gaimster,
And like it is, in plaie sheele hazard it,
For if report but blasen her aright,
Shees a franke gaimster, and inclinde to play, Ho *Piston?*

            Enter Piston.

  Pist. Heere sir, what would you with me,
  Era, Desire *Guelpio* & signior *Iulio* come speake with me
And bid them bring some store of crownes with them,
And sirra, prouide me foure Visards,
Foure Gownes, a boxe, and a Drumme,
For I intend to go in mummery,
    Pist. I will sir.   *Exit* Piston.
    Erast. Ah vertuous Lampes of euer turning heauens,
Incline her minde to play, and mine to win,
Nor do I couet but what is mine owne,
Then shall I let *Perseda* vnderstand,
How iealousie had armd her tongue with malice,
Ah were she not *Perseda* whom my heart,
No more can slie, then iron can Adamant,
Her late vnkindnes would haue chaunged my minde.
       Enter Guelpio *and* Iulio *and* Piston.
  Guelp. How now *Erastus*, wherein may we pleasure thee?
  Erast. Sirs thus it is, we must in mummerie,
Vnto *Lucina,* neither for loue nor hate,
But if we can, to win the chaine she weares,
For though I haue some interest therein,
Fortune may make me maister of mine owne,
Rather then ile seeke iustice gainst the Dame,
But this assure your selues it must be mine,
By game, or change, by one deuise or other.
The rest ile tell you when our sport is doone.
    Iulio. VVhy then lets make vs ready and about it,
    Erast. VVhat store of Crownes haue you brought?
    Guel. Feare not for money man, ile beare the Boxe,
    Iulio, I haue some little replie, if neede require.
    Pist. I but heare you Maister, was not he a foole?

                               That

930

940

950

That went to fhoote, and left his arrowes behinde him.

 Eraft. Yes, but what of that?

 Pift. Mary that you may loofe your money,

And go without the chaine, vnleffe you carrie falfe dice.

 Guel. Mas the foole fayes true, lets haue fome got.

 Pift. Nay I vfe not to go without a paire of falfe Dice.

Heere are tall men and little men.

 Iulio. Hie men and low men, thou wouldft fay.

 Eraft. Come firs lets go, Drumfler pray for me,

And ile reward thee : and firra *Piftrn*,

Mar not our fport with your foolery.

 Pift. I warrant you fir, they get not one wife word of me.

     Sound vp the Drum to Lucinaes *doore.*

    Enter Lucina.

 Luci. I marrie, this fhowes that Charleman is come,

What fhall we play heere? content,

Since Signior *Ferdinand* will haue it fo.

  Then they play, and when fhe hath loft her gold, Eraftus

   pointed to her Chaine, and then fhe fayd:

I were it *Cleopatraes* vnion :

   Then Eraftus *winneth the Chaine, and loofeth his gould.*

    And Lucina *faies.*

Signior *Fernando*, I am fure tis you,

And Gentlemen, vnmaske ere you depart,

That I may know to whom my thankes is due,

For this fo courteous and vnlookt for fport :

No wilt not be, then fup with me to morrow,

Well then ile looke for you, till then farewell.

     Exit Lucina.

 Eraft. Gentlemen, each thing hath forted to our wifh,

She tooke me for *Fernando*, markt you that :

Your gould fhall be repairde with double thankes,

And fellow Drumfler, ile reward you well.

 Pift. But is there no reward for my falfe dice ?

 Eraft. Yes fir, a garded fute from top to toe.

    Enter Ferdinando.

 Ferdi. Dafell mine eyes, or ift *Lucinas* chaine,

    D 3   Falfe

False treacher, lay downe the chaine that thou haſt ſtole,
   Eraſt. He lewdly lyes that cals me treacherous.
   Fern. That lye my weapon ſhall put downe thy throate:
         Then Eraſtus *ſlaies* Ferdinando.
   Iulio. Flie *Eraſtus,* ere the Gouernour haue any newes,
Whoſe neere alye he was, and cheefe delight,
   Eraſt. Nay Gentlemen, flie you and ſaue your ſelues,
Leaſt you pertake the hardnes of my fortune.
         Exeunt Guelpio *and* Iulio.
Ah fickle and blind guidreſſe of the world,
What pleaſure haſt thou in my miſerie?
Waſt not enough when I had loſt the Chaine,
Thou didſt bereaue me of my deareſt loue,
But now when I ſhould repoſeſſe the ſame,
To croſſe me with this hapleſſe accedent:
Ah if but time and place would giue me leaue,
Great eaſe it were for me to purge my ſelfe,
And to acuſe fell *Fortune, Loue* and *Death.*
For all theſe three conſpire my tragedie,
But danger waites vppon my words and ſteps,
I dare not ſtay, for if the Gouernour
Surpriſe me heere, I die by marſhall law,
Therefore I go. But whether ſhall I go?
If into any ſtay adioyning Rhodes,
They will betray me to *Phyllippos* hands,
For loue, or gaine, or flatterie.
To Turkie muſt I go, the paſſage ſhort,
The people warlike, and the king renownd,
For all heroyicall and kingly vertues,
Ah hard attempt, to tempt a foe for ayde,
Neceſſitie yet ſayes it muſt be ſo,
Or ſuffer death for *Ferdinandos* death,
Whom honors title forſt me to miſdoe,
By checking his outragious inſolence.
Piſton, heere take this chaine, and giue it to *Perſeda,*
And let her know what hath befallen me,
When thou haſt deliuered it, take ſhip and follow me,
                   I will

1000
1010
1020
1030

I will be in Constantinople.
Farewell my countrie dearer then my life;
Farewell sweete friends, dearer then countrey soyle,
Farewell *Perseda*, dearest of them all,
Dearer to me, then all the world besides.

                  Exit Erastus.

Pist. Now am I growing into a doubtfull agonie
What I were best to do, to run away with this Chaine,
Or deliuer it, and follow my maister.
If I deliuer it and follow my maister, I shall haue thanks,
But they will make me neuer the fatter,
If I run away with it, I may liue vpon credit
All the while I weare this chaine,
Or dominere with the money when I haue sold it,
Hetherto all goes well, but if I be taken,
I marry sir, then the case is altered, I and haltered to,
Of all things I do not loue to preach
With a haulter about my neck,
Therfore for this once, ile be honest against my will,
Perseda shall haue it, but before I go, ile be so bolde
As to diue into this Gentlemans pocket, for good luck sake,
If he deny me not: how say you sir, are you content?
A plaine case, *Qui tacet confitiri videtur.*

             Enter Phylippo *and* Iulio.

   Iulio. See where his body lyes.
   Philip. I, I, I see his body all to soone,
What barbarous villaine ist that rifles him.
Ah *Ferdinand*, the stay of my old age,
And cheefe remainder of our progenie,
Ah louing cousen how art thou misdone,
By false *Erastus*, ah no by treacherie,
For well thy valour hath beene often tride,
But whilst I stand and weepe, and spend the time
In fruitlesse plaints, the murtherer will escape,
VVithout reuenge, sole salue for such a sore,
Say villaine, wherefore didst thou rifle him?

                                     Pist.

*Piʃt.*Faith ʃir for pure good will,
Seeing he was going towards heauen,
I thought to ʃee, if he had a paʃport to S. *Nicholas* r no, 1070
  *Philip.*Some ʃot he ʃeemes to be, twere pittie to hurt him:
Sirra canʃt thou tell who ʃlew this man?
  *Piʃt.*I ʃir very well, it was my maiʃter *Eraʃtus.*
  *Philp.*Thy maiʃter, and whether is he gone now?
  *Piʃt.*To fetch the Sexten to burie him I thinke.
  *Phil.*Twere pittie to impriʃon ʃuch a ʃot,
  *Piʃt.*Now it fits my wiʃdome to counterfeit the foole.
  *Phil.*Come hether ʃirra, thou knoweʃt me
For the Gouernour of the cittie, dooʃt thou not? 1080
  *Piʃt.*I forʃooth ʃir.
  *Phil.*Thou art a bondman, and wouldʃt faine be free?
  *Piʃt.*I forʃooth ʃir.
  *Phil.*Then do but this, and *I* will make thee free,
And rich wiihall, learne where *Eraʃtus* is,
And bring me word, and ile reward thee well.
  *Piʃt.*That I will ʃir, I ʃhall finde you at the Caʃtle, ʃhall I
  *Phil.*Yes. (not?
  *Piʃt.*Why ile be here, as ʃoone as euer I come againe.
                Exit Piʃton. 1090
  *Phil.*But for aʃʃurance that he may not ʃcape,
VVeele lay the ports and hauens round about,
And let a proclamation ʃtraight be made,
That he that can bring foorth the murtherer,
Shall haue three thouʃand Duckets for his paines,
My ʃelfe will ʃee the body borne from hence,
And honored with Balme and funerall. *Exit.*
            Enter Piʃton.
  *Piʃt.*God ʃends fortune to fooles.
Did you euer ʃee wiʃe man eʃcape as *I* haue done, 1100
I muʃt betraie my maiʃter: *I* but when can you tell?
            Enter Perʃeda.
See where *Perʃeda* comes, to ʃaue me a labour.
After my moʃt hearty commendations,
This is to let you vnderʃtand,

                              That

That my maifter was in good health at the fending hereof,
Yours for euer and euer and euer.
In moft humble wife *Pifton.*

Then he deliuered her the Chaine.

1110 *Perfe.* This makes me thinke that I haue been to cruell,
How got he this from of *Lucinas* arme?

Pift. Faith in a mummery, and a paire of falfe dice,
I was one of the mummers my felfe, fimple as I ftand here.

Perfe. I rather thinke it coft him very deare.

Pift. I fo it did, for it coft *Ferdinando* his life.

Perfe. How fo?

Pyft. After we had got the chaine in mummery,
And loft our box in counter cambio,
My maifter wore the chaine about his necke,
1120 Then *Ferdinando* met vs on the way,
And reuild my maifter, faying he ftole the chaine,
With that they drew, & there *Ferdinando* had the prickado.

Perfe. And whether fled my poore *Eraftus* then?

Pift. To *Conftantinople* whether I muft follow him,
But ere he went, with many fighes and teares,
He deliuered me the chaine, and bad me giue it you,
For perfect argument that he was true,
And you too credulous.

Perfe. Ah ftay, no more, for *I* can heere no more.

1130 *Pift.* And I can fing no more.

Perfe. My hart had armd my tongue with iniury,
To wrong my friend, whofe thoughts were euer true,
Ah poore *Eraftus* how thy ftarres maling:
Thou great commander of the fwift wingd winds,
And dreadfull *Neptune* bring him backe againe,
But *Eolus* and *Neptune* let him go,
For heere is nothing but reuenge and death,
Then let him go, ile fhortly follow him,
Not with flow failes, but with loues goulden winges,
1140 My fhip fhall be borne with teares, and blowne with fighes
So will I foare about the Turkifh land,
Vntill I meete *Eraftus* my fweete freend.

E   And

33

And then and there,fall downe amid his armes,
And in his bosome there power foorth my soule,
For satiffaction of my trespasse past.

Enter Bafilisco,*armde.*

Baſi. Faire Loue,according vnto thy commaund,
I seeke *Eraſtus* and will combate him.

Perſe. I seeke him,finde him,bring him to my sight,
For till we meete,my hart shall want delight.

Exit Perſeda.

Baſi. My petty fellow, where haſt thou hid thy maiſter,

Piſt. Marrie sir in an Armorours shop,
Where you had not beſt go to him.

Baſi. Why so,I am in honour bound to combat him,

Piſt. I sir,but he knowing your fierce conditions,
Hath planted a double cannon in the doore,
Ready to difcharge it vppon you,when you go by,
I tell you for pure good will.

Baſi. In Knightly curteſie,I thanke thee,
But hopes the coyſtrell to eſcape me so,
Thinkes he bare cannon shot can keepe me back:
Why wherfore ſerues my targe of proofe,but for the bullet
That once put by,I roughly come vpon him,
Like to the wings of lightning from aboue,
I with a martiall looke aſtonish him,
Then fals he downe poore wretch vpon his knee,
And all to late, repents his ſurquedry.
Then do I take him on my fingers point,
And thus I beare him thorough euery ſtreete,
To be a laughing ſtock to all the towne.
That done,I lay him at my miſtres feete,
For her to giue him doome of life or death.

Piſt. I but heere you sir, I am bound
In paine of my maiſters difpleaſure,
To haue about at cuffes,afore you and I part,

Baſi. Ha,ha,ha,Eagles are chalenged by paltry flyes,
Thy folly giues thee priuiledge,begon,begon,

Piſt. No,no sir,I muſt haue about with you sir thats flat,

Leaſt

1150

1160

1170

That for retaining one so vertuous,
Least my maister turne me out of seruice.

Basi. Why, art thou wearie of thy life?

Pist. No by my faith sir.

Basi. Then fetch thy weapons, and with my single fist,
Ile combat thee, my body all vnarm'd.

Pist. Why lend me thine, and saue me a labour.

Basi. I tell thee, if *Alcides* liued this day,
He could not weild my weapons.

Pist. Why wilt thou stay till I come againe?

Basi. I vpon my honour.

Pist. That shall be when I come from Turkey. *Exit* Pist.

Basi, Is this little desperate fellow gon,
Doubtlesse he is a very tall fellow,
And yet it were disgrace to all my chiualrie,
To combate one so base:
Ile send some Crane to combate with the Pigmew,
Not that I feare, but that I scorne to fight. *Exit* Basilis.

Enter Chorus.

Loue. Fortune thou madest *Fernando* finde the chaine,
But yet by *Loues* instruction he was taught,
To make a present of it to his Mistris,

For. But *Fortune* would not let her keepe it long.

Loue. Nay rather *Loue,* by whose suggisted power,
Erastus vsde such dice, as being false,
Ran not by *Fortune,* but necessitie.

Fort. Meane time I brought *Fernando* on the way,
To see and chalenge what *Lucina* lost.

Death. And by that chalenge I abridgde his life,
And forst *Erastus* into banishment,
Parting him from his loue, in spight of *Loue,*

Loue. But with my goulden winges ile follow him,
And giue him aide and succour in distresse.

Fort. And doubt not to, but *Fortune* will be there,
And crosse him too, and sometimes flatter him,
And lift him vp, and throw him downe againe.

E 2 *Death,*

Death. And here and there in ambush *Death* will stand,
To marre what *Loue* or *Fortune* takes in hand. *Exeunt.*

Enter Solyman *and* Brusor, *with Janisaries.*

Soly. How long shall *Soliman* spend his time,
And waste his dayes in fruitlesse obsequies,
Ads but a trouble to my brothers ghost:
Perhaps my greefe and long continuall moane.
Which but for me would now haue tooke their rest,
Then farewell sorrow, and now reuenge draw neere.
In controuersie touching the Ile of Rhodes,
My brothers dyde, on Rhodes ile he reuengd,
Now tell me *Brusor* whats the newes at Rhodes?
Hath the yong prince of *Cipris* married
Cornelia, daughter to the Gouernour.

Bru. He hath my Lord, with the greatest pompe,
That ere I saw at such a festiuall.

Soli. What greater then at our coronation?

Bru. Inferiour to that onely.

Soli. At tilt, who woone the honor of the day?

Bru. A worthie Knight of Rhodes, a matchlesse man,
His name *Erastus*, not twentie yeares of age,
Not tall, but well proportioned in his lims,
I neuer saw, except your excellence,
A man whose presence more delighted me,
And had he worshipt Mahomet for Christ,
He might haue borne me through out all the world,
So well I loued and honoured the man.

Soli. These praises *Brusor* touch me to the heart,
And makes me wish that I had beene at Rhodes,
Vnder the habit of some errant knight,
Both to haue seene and tride his valour.

Brusor. You should haue seene him foile and ouerthrow,
All the Knights that there incountred him.

Soli. What ere he be, euen for his vertues sake,
I wish that fortune of our holy wars,
Would yeeld him prisoner vnto *Soliman*.

That

1220

1230

1240

1250

We may our selues be famd for vertues,
But let him passe, and *Brusor* tell me now,
How did the Christians vse onr Knights?
 Bru. As if that we and they had beene on sect,
 Soli. What thinkst thou of their valour and demeanor?
 Bru. Braue men at armes, and friendly out of armes,
Courteous in peace, in battell dangerous,
Kinde to their foes, and liberall to their friends,
And all in all, their deedes heroicall.
 Soli. Then tell me *Brusor*, how is Rhodes fenst,
For eyther Rhodes shall be braue *Solymans*,
Or cost me more braue Souldiers
Then all that Ile will beare.
 Brusor. Their fleete is weake:
Their horsse, I deeme them fiftie thousand strong,
Their footemen more, well exercised in war,
And as it seemes, they want no needfull vittaile.
 Soli. How euer Rhodes be fencd by sea or land,
It eyther shall be mine, or burie me:
    Enter Erastus.
Whats he that thus bouldly enters in?
His habite argues him a Christian,
 Erast. I worthie Lord a forlorne Christian.
 Soli. Tell me man, what madnes brought thee hether?
 Erast. Thy vertuous fame, and mine owne miserie.
 Soli. What miserie? speake, for though you Christians,
Account our Turkish race but barbarous,
Yet haue we eares to heare a iust complaint,
And iustice to defend the innocent,
And pitie, to such as are in pouertie,
And liberall hands to such as merit bountie,
 Bru. My gratious Soueraigne, as this Knight,
Seemes by greefe tyed to silence,
So his deserts binds me to speake for him.
This is *Erastus* the Rhodian worthie,
The flower of chiualrie and curtesie,
 Soli. Is this the man that thou hast so describde?
    E 3   Stand

Stand vp faire knight, that what my heart desires,   1290
Mine eyes may view with pleasnre and delight,
This face of thine should harbour no deceit.
Erastus ile not yet vrge to know the cause,
That brought thee hether,
Least with the discourse, thou shouldst afflict thy selfe,
And crosse the fulnes of my ioyfull passion,
But that we are assurde,
Heauens brought thee hether for our benefit,
Know thou that Rhodes, nor all that Rhodes containes,
Shall win thee from the side of *Soliman*,
If we but finde thee well inclind to vs.   1300

 Erast. If any ignoble or dishonourable thoughts,
Should dare attempt, or but creepe neere my heart:
Honour should force disdaine to roote it out,
As ayre bred Eagles, if they once perceiue,
That any of their broode but close their sight,
When they should gase against the glorious Sunne,
They straight way sease vpon him with their talents,
That on the earth it may vntimely die,
For looking but a scue at heauens bright eye.

 Soli. *Erastus*, to make thee well assurde,   1310
How well thy speach and presents liketh vs,
Aske what thou wilt, it shall be graunted thee.

 Erast. Then this my gratious Lord is all I craue,
That being banisht from my natiue soile,
I may haue libertie to liue a Christian.

 Soly. I that, or any thing thou shalt desire,
Thou shalt be Captaine of our Ianisaries,
And in our counsell shalt thou sit with vs,
And be great *Solimans* adopted freend.

 Erast. The least of these surpasse my best desart,   1320
Vnlesse true loyaltie may seeme desart.

 Soli. *Erastus*, now thou hast obtaind thy boone,
Denie not *Soliman* this owne request;
A vertuous enuie pricks me with desire,
To trie thy valour, say art thou content?

          Erast.

Eraſt. I, if my Soueraigne ſay content, I yeeld.

Soli. Then giue vs Swords and Targets,
And now *Eraſtus* thinke me thine enemie,
But euer after thy continuall friend,
And ſpare me not, for then thou wrongſt my honour.

Then they fight, and Eraſtus *ouercomes* Solyman.

Nay, nay *Eraſtus*, throw not downe thy weapons,
As if thy force did faile, it is enough
That thou haſt conquered *Soliman* by ſtrength,
By curteſie let *Soliman* conquer thee.
And now from armes to counſell ſit thee downe:
Before thy comming I vowd to conquer Rhodes,
Say wilt thou be our Lejutenant there,
And further vs in manage of theſe wars?

Eraſt. My gratious Soueraigne, without preſumption,
If poore *Eraſtus* may once more intreat,
Let not great *Solimans* commaund,
To whoſe beheſt I vowe obedience,
Inforce me ſheath my ſlaughtering blade,
In the deere bowels of my countrimen:
And were it not that *Soliman* hath ſworne,
My teares ſhould plead for pardon to that place:
I ſpeake not this to ſhrinke away for feare,
Or hide my head in time of dangerous ſtormes,
Imploy me elſe where in thy forraine wars,
Againſt the Perſians or the barbarous Moore,
Eraſtus will be formoſt in the battell.

Soli. Why fauourſt thou thy countrimen ſo much,
By whoſe crueltie thou art exylde?

Eraſt. Tis not my countrey, but *Phylippos* wrath,
It muſt be tould, for *Ferdinandos* death,
Whom I in honours cauſe haue reft of life,

Soli. Nor ſuffer this or that to trouble thee,
Thou ſhalt not neede *Phylippo* nor his Ile,
Nor ſhalt thou war againſt thy Countrimen,
I like thy vertue in refuſing it,
But that our oath may haue his currant ccurſe,

Eruſor

Brusor, goe leuie men,
Prepare a fleete, to assault and conquer Rhodes,
Meane time *Erastus* and I will striue,
By mutuall kindnes to excell each other.
Brusor be gon, and see not *Soliman*,
Till thou hast brought Rhodes in subiection. *Exit* Brusor.
And now *Erastus* come and follow me.
Where thou shalt see what pleasures and what sports,
My Minions and my Euenukes can deuise,   1370
To driue away this melancholly moode.   *Exit* Soliman.
                    Enter Piston.
   Pist. Oh maister, see where I am,
   Erast. Say *Piston* whats the newes at Rhodes,
   Pist. Colde and comfortlesse for you,
Will you haue them all at once ?
   Erastus. I.
   Pist. Why the Gouernour will hang you & he catch you.
Ferdinando is buried, your friends commend them to you: 1380
Perseda hath the chaine, and is like to die for sorrow.
   Erast. I thats the greefe, that we are parted thus,
Come follow me and I will heare the rest,
For now I must attend the Emperour.   *Exeunt.*

                    Enter Perseda, Lucina, *and* Basilisco.
   Perse. Accursed Chaine, vnfortunate *Perseda.*
   Luci. Accursed Chaine, vnforrunate *Lucina,*
My friend is gone, aud I am desolate.
   Perse. My friend is gone, and I am desolate,
Returne him backe faire starres or let me die.   1390
   Luci. Returne him back faire heauens, or let me die,
For what was he but comfort of my life ?
   Perse. For what was he but comfort of my life?
But why was I so carefull of the Chaine.
   Luci. But why was I so carelesse of the chaine,
Had I not lost it, my friend had not beene slaine.
   Perse. Had I not askt it, my friend had not departed,
His parting is my death.
                              Luci.

*Luci.*His deaths my liues departing,

And here my tongue dooth stay , with swolne harts greefe,

*Per.*And here my swolne harts greef doth stay my tongue.

*Basi.*For whom weepe you ?

*Luci.*Ah,for *Fernandos* dying.

Basi. For whom mourne you?

Perse. Ah, for *Erastus* flying,

Basi. Why Lady is not *Basilisco* here ?

Why Lady dooth not *Basilisco* liue ?

Am not I worth both these for whom you mourne:

Then take one halfe of me ,and cease to weepe,

Or if you gladly would inioy me both,

Ile serue the one by day,the other by night,

And I will pay you both your sound delight.

*Luci.*Ah how vnpleasant is mirth to melancholy.

*Perse.*My heart is full,I cannot laugh at follie.

Exeunt Ladies.

Basi. See,see,*Lucina* hates me like a Toade,

Because that when *Erastus* spake my name,

Her loue *Fernando* died at the same,

So dreadfull is our name to cowerdice.

On the other side,*Perseda* takes it vnkindly,

That ere he went I brought not bound vnto her,

Erastus that faint hearted run away:

Alasse how could I,for his man no sooner

Informd him,that I sought him vp and downe,

But he was gon in twinckling of an eye:

But *I* will after my delitious loue,

For well I wot ,though she desemble thus,

And cloake affection with hir modestie,

With loue of me her thoughts are ouergone,

More then was *Phillis* with hir *Demophon.*   *Exit.*

Enter Philippo, *the Prince of* Cipris,*with*

other Souldiours.

Phil. Braue prince of Cipris, and our sonne in law,

Now there is little time to stand and talke,

The Turkes haue past our Gallies and are landed,

F   You

You with some men at armes shall take the Tower,
I with the rest will downe vnto the strane:
If we be beaten back weele come to you,
And here in spight of damned Turkes, weele gaine
A glorious death or famous victorie.   1440

    Cyp. About it then.   *Exeunt.*

          Enter Brusor, *and his Souldiers.*
    Bru. Drum sound a parle to the Citttzens.
          The Prince of Cypres on the walles.
    Cyp. What parle craues the Turkish at our hands.
    Bru. We come with mightie *Solimans* commaund,
Monarch and mightie Emperor of the world,
From East to Weast, from South, to Septentrion,
If you resist, expect what warre affordes,
Mischiefe, murther, bloud, and extremitie,   1450
What wilt thou yeeld and trie our clemencie?
Say *I*, or no; for we are peremtorie.
    Cyp. Your Lord vsurps in all that he posesseth,
And that great God which we do truly worship,
Shall strengthen vs against your insolence.
    Bru. Now if thou plead for mercie, tis to late:
Come fellow Souldiers, let vs to the breach,
Thats made already on the other side. *Exeunt, to the batel.*
         Phylippo and Cipris *are both slaine.*

    Enter Brusor, *with Souldiers, hauing* Guelpio, Iulio, *and*   1460
        Basilisco, *with* Perseda *and* Lucina *prisoners.*
    Bru. Now Rhodes is yoakt, and stoopes to *Soliman,*
There lies the Gouernour, and there his sonne:
Now let their soules tell sorrie tidings to their ancestors,
What millions of men opprest with ruine and scath,
The Turkish armies did in Christendome,
What say these prisoners, will they turne Turke, or no?
    Iulio. First *Iulio* will die ten thousand deaths.
    Guel. And *Guelpio*, rather then denie his Christ.
    Bru. Then stab the slaues, and send their soules to hell.   1470
         They stab Iulio *and* Guelpio.
                       Basi.

Baſ. I turne, I turne, oh ſaue my life I turne.

Bru. Forbeare to hurt him: when we land in Turkie
He ſhall be circumciſed and haue his rites.

Baſ. Thinke you I turne Turque,
For feare of ſeruile death thats but a ſport,
I faith ſir no:
Tis for *Perſeda* whom I loue ſo well,
That I would follow her, though ſhe went to hell.

Bru. Now for theſe Ladies: their liues priuiledge
Hangs on their beautie, they ſhall be preſerued,
To be preſented to great *Soliman,*
The greateſt honour Fortune could affoord.

Perſe. The moſt diſhonour that could ere befall. *Exeunt.*

Enter Chorus.

Lou. Now *Fortune,* what haſt thou done in this later paſſage

For. I plaſt *Eraſtus* in the fauour,
Of *Solyman* the Turkiſh Emperour.

Loue. Nay that was *Loue,* for *I* coucht my ſelfe
In poore *Eraſtus* eyes, and with a looke
Oreſpred with teares, bewitched *Solyman,*
Beſide I ſat on valiant *Bruſors* tongue,
To guide the praiſes of the herodian knight.
Then in the Ladies paſſions, I ſhowed my power,
And laſtly *Loue* made Baſiliſcos tougue,
To countercheck his hart by turning Turke,
And ſaue his life, in ſpight of deaths deſpight.

Death. How chance it then, that *Loue* and *Fortunes* power
Could neither ſaue *Philippo* nor his ſonne,
Nor *Guelpio,* nor ſignior *Iulio,*
Nor reſcue Rhodes from out the hands of *Death.*

For. Why *Bruſors* victorie was *Fortunes* gift.

Death. But had I ſlept, his conqueſt had beene ſmall.

Loue. Wherfore ſtay we, thers more behind, which proues
That though *Loue* winke, *Loues* not ſtarke blinde. *Exeunt.*

Enter Eraſtus *and* Piſton.

Piſt. Faith maiſter, me thinks you are vnwiſe.

F 2   That

That you weare not the high Sugerloafe hat,
And the gilded gowne the Emperour gaue you,

Erast. Peace foole, a sable weede fits discontent, Away, be   1510
Pist. Ile go prouide your supper,   (gon.
A shoulder of mutton, and neuer a Sallet.   *Exit* Piston.

Erast. I must confesse that *Solyman* is kinde,
Past all compare, and more then my desart,
But what helps gay garments, when the minds oprest,
What pleaseth the eye, when the sence is altered,
My heart is ouerwhelmd with thousand woes,
And melancholie leades my soule in triumphe,
No meruaile then if I haue little minde,   1520
Of rich imbroderie or costly ornaments,
Of honors titles, or of wealth, or gaine,
Of musick, viands, or of dainty dames,
No, no, my hope full long agoe was lost,
And Rhodes it selfe is lost, or els destroyde,
If not destroide, yet bound and captiuate,
If captiuate, then forst from holy faith :
If forst from faith, for euer miserable,
For what is misery, but want of God,
And God is lost, if faith be ouerthrowne.

Enter Solyman.

Solim. Why how now *Erastus*, alwaies in thy dumpes ?   1530
Still in black habite fitting funerall ?
Cannot my loue perswade thee from this moode,
Nor all my faire intreats and blandishments,
Wert thou my friend, thy minde would iumpe with mine,
For what are freends, but one minde in two bodies.
Perhaps thou doubts my friendships constancie,
Then doost thou wrong the measure of my loue,
Which hath no measure, and shall neuer end,
Come *Erastus* sit thee downe by me,
And ile impart to thee our *Brusors* newes,   1540
Newes to our honour, and to thy content:
The Gouernour is slaine that sought thy death.

E ast. A worthy man though not *Erastus* friend,

Soli.

44

Soli. The Prince of Cipris to, is likewise slaine.

Erast. Faire blossome, likely to haue proued good fruite,

Soli. Rhodes is taken, and all the men are slaine.
Except some few that turne to Mahomet.

Erast. I there it is, now all my freends are slaine,
And faire *Perseda* murtherd or deflowerd.
Ah gratious *Solyman* now show thy loue,
In not denying thy poore supplyant:
Suffer me not to stay here in thy presence,
But by my selfe lament me once for all,
Here if I stay, I must suppresse my teares,
And teares supprest will but increase my sorrow.

Soli. Go then, go spend thy mournings all at once,
That in thy presence *Soliman* may ioy.   *Exit* Erastus.
For hetherto haue I reaped little pleasure,
Well well Erastus, Rhodes may blesse thy birth,
For his sake onely, will I spare them more,
From spoile, pillage, and oppression,
Then *Alexander* spard warlike *Thebes*
For *Pindarus:* or then *Augustus*
Sparde rich *Alexandria* for *Arias* sake.

          Enter Brusor, Perseda, *and* Lucina.

Bru. My gratious Lord, reioyce in happinesse:
All Rhodes is yoakt, and stoopes to *Solyman.*

Soli. First thanks to heauen, and next to *Brusors* valour,
Which ile not guerdon with large promises,
But straight reward thee with a bounteous largesse:
But what two Christian Virgins haue we here?

Bru. Part of the spoile of Rhodes, which were preserued
To be presented to your mightinesse.

Soli. This present pleaseth more then all the rest,
And were their garments turnd from black to white,
I should haue deemd them *Iunoes* goodly Swannes,
Or *Venus* milke white Doues, so milde they are,
And so adornd with beauties miracle.
Heere *Brusor* this kinde Turtle shall be thine,
Take her and vse her at thy pleasure:

          F 3   But

But this kinde Turtle is for *Soliman*,
That her captiuitie may turne to blisse.
Faire lookes resembling *Phœbus* radiant beames,
Smooth forhead like the table of high *Ioue*,
Small pensild eye browes, like to glorious rainbowes,
Quicke lampelike eyes, like heauens two brightest orbes,
Lips of pure Corall breathing Ambrosie,
Cheekes, where the Rose and Lillie are incombate,
Necke whiter then the Snowie Apenines,
Brests like two ouerflowing Fountaines,
Twixt which a vale leads to the Elisian shades,
Where vnder couert lies the fount of pleasure,
Which thoughts may gesse, but tongue must not prophane.
A sweeter creature nature neuer made,
Loue neuer tainted *Solyman* till now,
Now faire Virgin let me heare thee speake.

   Perse. What can my tongue vtter, but greefe and death.
   Soli. The sound is hunnie, but the sence is gall :
Then sweeting blesse me with a cheerefull looke.

   Perse. How can mine eyes dart foorth a pleasant looke,
When they are stopt with flouds of flowing teares.

   Soli. If tongue with griefe, and eyes with teares be fild,
Say Virgin, how dooth thy heart admit,
The pure affection of great *Soliman*?

   Perse. My thoughts are like pillers of Adamant,
Too hard to take an new impression.

   Soli. Nay then I see my stooping makes her proud,
She is my vassaile, and I will commaund,
Coye Virgin knowest thou what offence it is,
To thwart the will and pleasure of a king ?
Why thy life is doone, if I but say the word.

   Perse. Why thats the period that my heart desires.
   Soli. And die thou shalt, vnlesse thou change thy minde.
   Perse. Nay then *Perseda* growes resolute,
Solimans thoughts and mine resemble,
Liues paralise that neuer can be ioyned.

   Soli. Then kneele thou downe,

And

And ar my hands receiue the stroake of death,
Domde to thy selfe by thine owne wilfulnes.

   Per. Strike, strike, thy words pierce deeper then thy blows.
   Soli. Brusor hide her, for her lookes withhould me,
              Then Brusor *hides her with a Lawne.*

O *Brusor* thou hast not hid her lippes,
For there sits *Venus* with *Cupid* on her knee,
And all the Graces smiling round about her,
So crauing pardon that I cannot strike.
   Bru. Her face is couerd ouer quite my Lord.
   Soli. Why, so.

O *Brusor*, seest thou not her milke white neck,
That Alablaster tower,
Twill breake the edge of my keene Semitor,
And peeces flying back will wound my selfe.
   Bru. Now she is all couered my Lord.
   Soli. Why now at last she dyes.
   Perse. O Christ receiue my soule.
   Soli. Harke *Brusor* she cals on Christ,
I will not send her to him,
Her wordes are musick,
The selfe same musick that in auncient dayes,
Brought *Alexander* from warre to banquetting,
And made him fall from skirmishing to kissing.
No my deare, Loue would not let me kill thee,
Though Maiestie would turne desire to wrath,
There lyes my sword, humbled at thy feete,
And I my selfe that gouerne many kings,
Intreate a pardon for my rash misdeede.
   Perse. Now *Soliman* wrongs his imperiall state,
But if thou loue me, and haue hope to win,
Graunt me one boone that I shall craue of thee,
   Soli. What ere it be, *Perseda* I graunt it thee,
   Perse. Then let me liue a Christian Virgin still,
Vnlesse my state shall alter by my will,
   Soli. My word is past, and I recall my passions,
What should he do with crowne and Emperie,

                           That

That cannot gouerne priuate fond affections,
Yet giue me leaue in honest sort to court thee,
To ease,though not to cure, my maladie:
Come sit thee downe vpon my right hand here,
This seate I keepe voide for another friend: 1660
Go Ianisaries call in your Gouernour,
So shall I ioy betweene two captiue friends,
And yet my selfe becaptiue to them both,
If friendships yoake were not at libertie:
See where he comes my other best beloued.

Enter Erastus.

*Perse.*My sweete and best beloued.

Erast. My sweete and best beloued:

Perse. For thee my deare *Erastus* haue I liued.

*Erast.*And I for thee,or els I had not liued. 1670

*Soli.*What words in affection doo I see?

*Erast.*Ah pardon me great *Soliman,*for this is she,
For whom I mourned more then for all Rhodes,
And from whose absence I deriued my sorrow.

*Perse.*And pardon me my Lord,for this is he,
For whom I thwarted *Solimans* intreats,
And for whose exile I lamented thus.

*Erast.*Euen from my childhood haue I tendred thee,
Witnesse the heauens of my vnfeined loue.

Soli. By this one accedent I well perceiue, 1680
That heauens and heauenly powers do manage loue,
I loue them both,*I* know not which the better,
They loue each other best,what then should follow,
But that *I* conquer both by my deserts,
And ioyne their hands,whose hearts are knit already,
Erastus and *Perseda* come you hether,
And both giue me your hands,
Erastus, none but thou couldst win *Perseda,*
*Perseda,*none but thou couldst win *Erastus*
From great *Soliman,*so well *I* loue you both: 1690
And now to turne late promises to good effect,
Be thou *Erastus* Gouernour of Rhodes,

By

48

By this thou shalt dismisse my garison.

    *Bruf.*Must he reape that for which I tooke the toile?
Come enuie then and sit in friendships seate,
How can I loue him that inioyes my right.

    *Solt.*Giue me a crowne, to crowne the bride withall,
                Then he crownes Perseda.
*Perseda,*for my sake weare this crowne:

1700
Now is she fairer then she was before,
This title so augments her beautie as the fire,
That lay with honours hand rackt vp in ashes,
Reuies againe to flames, the force is such,
Remooue the cause, and then the effect will die,
They must depart, or I shall not be quiet,
Eraftus and *Perseda,*meruaile not,
That all in hast I wish you to depart,
There is an vrgent cause, but priuie to my selfe,
Commaund my shipping for to waft you ouer.

1710
    *Era.*My gratious Lord, whē *Eraftus* doth forget this fauor,
Then let him liue abandond and forlorne.

    *Perfe.*Nor will *Perseda* slacke euen in her praiers
And still solicite God for *Soliman,*
Whose minde hath proued so good and gratious.

    Soli. Farewell *Eraftus,Perfeda* farewell to.   *Exeunt.*
Me thinks *I* should not part with two such friends,
The one so renownd for armes and curtesie,
The other so adornd with grace and modestie:
Yet of the two *Perseda* mooues me most,

1720
I and so mooues me, that I now repent,
That ere I gaue away my hearts desire,
What was it but abuse of Fortunes gift,
And therefore Fortune now will be reuengde.
What was it but abuse of loues commaund,
And therefore mightie Loue will be reuengd:
What was it but abuse of heauens that gaue her me,
And therefore angrie heauens will be reuengd:
Heauens, Loue, and Fortune, all three haue decreed,
That I shall loue her still, and lack her still,

                  G   . Lik:

Like euer thirfting wretched *Tantalus*?   1730
Foolifh *Soliman*, why did I ftriue,
To do him kindnes, and vndoe my felfe?
Well gouernd friends do firft regard themfelues.
   Bru. I now occafion ferues to ftumble him,
That thruft his fickle in my harueft corne,
Pleafeth your Maieftie to heare *Brufor* fpeake.
   Soli. To one paft cure, good counfell comes too late,
Yet fay thy minde.
   Bru. With fecret letters woe her, and with gifts,
   Soli. My lines and gifts will but returne my fhame.   1740
   Luci. Here me my Lord, let me go ouer to Rhodes,
That I may plead in your affections caufe,
One woman may do much to win another.
   Soli. Indeede *Lucina* were her husband from her,
She happely might be woone by thy perfwades,
But whilft he liues there is no hope in her.
   Bru. Why liues he then to greeue great *Soliman*,
This onely remaines, that you confider,
In two extreames the leaft is to be chofen,
If fo your life depend vpon her loue,   1750
And that her loue depends vpon his life,
Is it not better that *Eraftus* die
Ten thoufand deaths, then *Soliman* fhould perifh?
   Soli. I faift thou fo? why then it fhall be fo,
But by what meanes fhall poore *Eraftus* die?
   Bru. This fhall be the meanes,
Ile fetch him backe againe,
Vnder couler of great confequence,
No fooner fhall he land vpon our fhore,
But witnes fhall be ready to accufe him,   1760
Of treafon doone againft your mightines,
And then he fhall be doomd by marfhall law,
   Soli. Oh fine deuife, *Brufor* get thee gone,
Come thou againe, but let the lady ftay,
To win *Perfeda* to my will, meane while,
Will I prepare the iudge and witneffes,

And

And if this take effect, thou shalt be Viceroy,
And faire *Lucina* Queene of *Tripolie*,
Brusor be gone, for till thou come I languish.

       Exeunt Brusor *and* Lucina.

And now to ease my troubled thoughts at last,
I will go sit among my learned Euenukes,
And here them play, and see my minions dance,
For till that *Brusor* bring me my desire,
I may asswage, but neuer quench loues fire. *Exit.*

     Enter Basilisco.

 Basi. Since the expugnation of the Rhodian Ile,
Me thinkes a thousand yeares are ouerpast,
More for the lack of my *Persedas* presence,
Then for the losse of Rhodes that paltry Ile,
Or for my friends that there were murthered,
My valour euery where shall purchase friends,
And where a man liues well, there is his countrie.
Alas the Christians are but very shallow,
In giuing iudgement of a man at armes,
A man of my desert and excellence.
The Turkes whom they account for barbarous,
Hauing forehard of Basiliscoes worth,
A number vnder prop me with their shoulders,
And in procession bare me to the Church,
As I had beene a second Mahomet,
I fearing they would adore me for a God,
Wisely informd them that I was but man,
Although in time perhaps I might aspire,
To purchase Godhead, as did *Hercules,*
I meane by doing wonders in the world :
Amidst their Church they bound me to a piller,
And to make triall of my valiancie,
They lopt a collop of my tendrest member.
But thinke you Basilisco squicht for that,
Euen as a Cowe for tickling in the horne,
That doone, they set me on a milke white Asse,
Compassing me with goodly ceremonies,

      G 2   That

That day me thought, I sat in *Pompeyes* Chaire,
And view'd the Capitoll, and was Romes greatest glorie.

Enter Piston.

Pist. I would my maister had left
Some other to be his agent here:
Faith I am wearie of the office alreadie,
What Seigniour *Tremomundo*,
That rid a pilgrimage to beg cakebread.

Baſ. O take me not vnprouided, let me fetch my weapons.

Piſt. Why I meant nothing but a *Baſolus Manus.*

Baſi. No, didſt thou not meane to giue me the priuie ſtab?

Piſt. No by my troth ſir.

Baſ. Nay if thou hadſt, I had not feard thee I,
I tell thee my skin holds out Piſtoll proofe.

Piſt. Piſtoll proofe? ile trie if it will hold out pin prooue,
Then he pricks him with a pin.

Baſ. O ſhoote no more great God I yeeld to thee.

Piſt. I ſee his skin is but piſtol profe from the girdle vpward
What ſuddaine agonie was that?

Ba. VVhy ſawſt thou not, how *Cupid* God of loue,
Not daring looke me in the marſhall face,
Came like a coward ſtealing after me,
And with his pointed dart prickt my poſteriors.

Piſt. Then here my opinion concerning that point,
The Ladies of Rhodes hearing that you haue loſt,
A capitoll part of your Lady ware,
Haue made their petition to Cupid,
To plague you aboue all other,
As one preiuditiall to their muliebritie,
Now ſir, *Cupid* ſeeing you alreadie hurt before,
Thinkes it a greater puniſhment to hurt you behind,
Therfore I would wiſh you to haue an eye to the back dore

Baſ. Sooth thou ſaieſt, I muſt be fencd behinde,
I'e hang my target there.

Piſt. Indeede that will ſerue to beare of ſome blowes,
VVhen you run away in a fraye.

Baſ. Sirra, ſirra, what art thou?

That

52

That thus incrochest vpon my familiaritie,
VVithout speciall admittance.

 Pist. VVhy do you not know me? I am *Erastus* man,

 Bas. VVhat art thou that pettie pigmie,
That chalnegedme at Rhodes:
VVhom I refusd to combat for his minoritie,
Where is *Erastus* I owe him chastisment in *Perseda's* quarrel.

 Pist. Do not you know that they are all friends,
And *Erastus* maryed to *Perseda*,
And *Erastus* made gouernour of Rhodes,
And I left heere to be their agent?

 Bas. O cœlum, O terra, O maria Neptune,
Did I turne Turke to follow her so far,

 Pist. The more shame for you.

 Bas. And is she linkt in liking with my foe?

 Pist. Thats because you were out of the way.

 Bas. O wicked Turque for to steale her hence.

 Pist. O wicked turne coate that would haue her staye.

 Bas. The truethis, ile be a Turke no more.

 Pist. And I feare thou wilt neuer prooue good christian.

 Bas. I will after to take reuenge.

 Pist. And ile stay heere about my maisters busines.

 Bas. Farewell Constantinople, I will to Rhodes. *Exit.*

 Pist. Farewell counterfeit foole,
God send him good shipping:
Tis noisd about, that *Brusor* is sent,
To fetch my maister backe againe,
I cannot be well till I heare the rest of the newes,
Therefore Ile about it straight. *Exit.*

Enter Chorus.

 Loue. Now *Fortune* what hast thou done in this latter act?

 Fort. I brought *Perseda* to the presence,
Of *Soliman* the Turkish Emperour,
And gaue *Lucina* into *Brusors* hands.

 Loue. And first I stunge them with consenting loue,
And made great *Soliman* sweete beauties thrall,
Humble himselfe at faire *Persedas* feete,

G 3   And

And made him praise loue and captiues beautie :
Againe,I made him to recall his passions,
And giue *Perseda* to *Erastus* hands,
And after make repentance of the deed.

    For. Meane time I fild *Erastus* sailes with winde,
And brought him home vnto his natiue land.

    Death. And I subornd *Brusor* with enuious rage,
To counsell *Soliman* to slay his friend,
Brusor is sent to fetch him back againe,
Marke well what followes,for the historie
Prooues me cheefe actor in this tragedie .   *Exeunt.*

Enter Erastus *and* Perseda.

    Erast. Perseda,these dayes are our dayes of ioy.
What could I more desire then thee to wife,
And that I haue : or then to gouerne Rhodes,
And that I doe,thankes to great *Soliman,*

    Perse. And thankes to gratious heauens,that so
Brought *Soliman* from worse to better,
For though I neuer tould it thee till now,
His heart was purpos'd once to do thee wrong.

    Erast. I that was before he knew thee to be mine,
But now *Perseda*,lets forget ould greefes ,
And let our studies wholie be imploid,
To worke each others blisse and hearts delight.

    Per. Our present ioyes will be so much the greater,
When as we call to minde forepassed greefes,
So singes the Mariner vpon the shore,
When he hath past the dangerous time of stormes:
But if my Loue will haue olde greefes forgot,
They shall lie buried in *Persedas* brest.

Enter Brusor *and* Lucina.

    Erast. Welcome Lord *Brusor.*
    Perse. And *Lucina* to.
    Bru. Thankes Lord gouernour.
    Luci. And thankes to you Madame.

Erast.

54

Eraſt. What haſtie news brings you ſo ſoone to Rhodes?
Although to me you neuer come to ſoone.

Bru. So it is my Lord, that vpon great affaires,
Importuning health and wealth of *Soliman,*
His highnes by me intreateth you,
As euer you reſpect his future loue,
Or haue regard vnto his curteſie,
To come your ſelfe in perſon and viſit him,
Without inquirie what ſhould be the cauſe.

Eraſt. VVere there no ſhips to croſſe the Seas withall,
My armes ſhould frame mine oares to croſſe the ſeas,
And ſhould the ſeas turne tide to force me backe,
Deſire ſhould frame me winges to flie to him,
I go *Perſeda* thou muſt giue me leaue.

Perſe. Though loth, yet *Solimans* command preuailes.

Luci. And ſweete *Perſeda* I will ſtay with you,
From *Bruſor* my beloued, and Ile want him,
Till he bring backe *Eraſtus* vnto you.

Eraſt. Lord *Bruſor* come tis time that we were gon.

Bru. *Perſeda* farewell, be not angrie,
For that I carry thy beloued from thee,
VVe will returne with all ſpeede poſſible,
And thou *Lucina,* vſe *Perſeda* ſo,
That for my carrying of *Eraſtus* hence,
She curſe me not, and ſo farewell to both.

Per. Come *Lucina* lets in, my heart is full.   *Exeunt.*

Enter Soliman, Lord marſhall, the two witneſſes,
      and Ianiſaries.

Soli. Lord marſhall, ſee you handle it cunningly,
And when *Eraſtus* comes our periurd friend,
See he be condemnd by marſhall law,
Heere will I ſtand to ſee and not be ſeene.

Marſhall. Come fellowes ſee when this matter comes in
You ſtagger not: and Ianiſaries,   (queſtion,
See that your ſtrangling cordes be readie.

Soli. Ah that *Perſeda* were not halfe ſo faire,

                                                        Or

Or that *Soliman* were not so fond,
Or that *Perseda* had some other loue,
Whose death might saue my poore *Erastus* life,

    Enter Brusor, *and* Erastus.

See where he comes, whome though I deerely loue,
Yet must his bloud be spilt for my behoofe,
Such is the force of morrow burning loue.

 Marshall. Erastus, Lord Gouernour of Rhodes,
I arrest you in the Kings name.

  Erast. What thinks Lord *Brusor* of this strange arrest,
Hast thou intrapt me to this tretcherie:
Intended well I wot without the leaue
Or licence of my Lord great *Soliman*.

  Bru. Why then appeale to him, where thou shalt know
And be assured that I betray thee not.

  Soli. Yes, thou, and I, and all of vs betray him.

  Mar. No, no, in this case no appeale shall serue.

  Era. Why then to thee, or vnto any else,
I heere protest by heauens vnto you all,
That neuer was there man more true or iust,
Or in his deeds more loyall and vpright,
Or more louing, or more innocent,
Than *I* haue bene to gratious *Soliman*,
Since first *I* set my feet on Turkish land.

  Soli. My selfe would be his witnesse if I durst,
But bright *Persedaes* beautie stops my tongue.

  Mar. Why sirs, why face to face expresse you not,
The treasons you reueald to *Soliman?*

  Witnesses. That very day *Erastus* went from hence,
He sent for me into his Cabinet,
And for that man that is of my profession.

  Eras. I neuer saw them *I* vntill this day.

  Witnesse His Cabine dore fast shut, he first began
To question vs of all sorts of fire-workes,
Wherein, when we had fully resolued him,
VVhat might be done, he spredding on the boord,
A huge heape of our imperiall coyne,

             All

All this is yours quoth he, if you consent,
To leaue great *Soliman* and serue in Rhodes.

Mar. Why that was treason, but onwards with the rest.

Enter Piston.

Pist. What haue we heer, my maister before the marshall?

Witn. We said not I, nor durst we say him nay,
Bicause we were already in his gallyes,
But seemd content to flie with him to Rhodes,
With that he purst the gould, and gaue it vs.
The rest I dare not speake it is so bad.   (them

Erast. Heauens heer you this, and drops not vengeance on
The other wit. The rest, and worst, will I discourse in briefe,
Will you consent quoth he to fire the fleete,
That lies hard by vs heere in *Bossphoron*,
For be it spoke in secret heere quoth he,
Rhodes must no longer beare the turkish yoake,
We said the taske might easilie be performd,
But that we lackt such drugs to mixe with powder,
As were not in his gallyes to be got,
At this he lept for ioy, swearing and promisiug,
That our reward should be redoubled:
We came aland not minding for to returne,
And as our duty and aleageance bound vs,
We made all knowne vnto great *Soliman*,
But ere we could summon him a land,
His ships were past a kenning from the shore,
Belike he thought we had bewrayd his treasons.

Marsh. That all is true that heere you haue declard,
Both lay your hands vpon the Alcaron.

1. *Wit.* Foule death betide me if I sweare not true,
2. *Wit.* And mischiefe light on me, if I sweare false.

Soli. Mischiefe and death shall light vpon you both.

Mar. Erastus thou seest what witnes hath produced against
What answerest thou vnto their accusations?   (thee,

Erast. That these are Synons and my selfe poore Troy.

Mar. Now it resteth, I appoint thy death,
Wherein thou shalt confesse ile fauour thee,

                    H   For

57

For that thou wert beloued of *Soliman*,
Thou shalt foorthwith be bound vnto that post,
And strangled as our Turkish order is.

    Pist. Such fauour send all Turkes I pray God.

    Erast. I see this traine was plotted ere I came,
What bootes complaining wheres no remedy:
Yet giue me leaue before my life shall end,
To moane *Perseda*, and accuse my friend.

    Soli. O vniust *Soliman*, O wicked time,
Where filthie lust must murther honest loue.

    Marsh. Dispatch, for our time limited is past.

    Erast. Alas, how can he but be short, whose tongue
Is fast tide with galling sorrow.
Farewell *Perseda*, no more but that for her:
Inconstant *Soliman*, no more but that for him,
Vnfortunate *Erastus*, no more but that for me:
Loe this is al. & thus I leaue to speake. *Then they strangle him*

    Pist. Marie sir this is a faire warning for me to get me gon.   2040

                          Exit Piston.

    Soli. O saue his life, if it be possible,
I will not loose him for my kingdomes worth,
Ah poore *Erastus* art thou dead already,
What bould presumer durst be so resolued,
For to bereaue *Erastus* life from him,
Whose life to me was dearer then mine owne,
VVast thou and thou, Lord marshall bring them hether,
And at *Erastus* hand let them receiue,
The stroake of death, whom they haue spoild of life:
VVhat is thy hand to weake? then mine shall helpe,   2050
To send them downe to euerlasting night,
To waite vpon thee through eternall shade,
Thy soule shall not go mourning hence alone:
Thus die and thus, for thus you murtherd him,
              Then he kils the two Ianisaries, that kild Erastus.
But soft me thinkes he is not satisfied,
The breath doth murmure softly from his lips,
And bids me kill those bloudie witnesses,

                                    By

By whose treacherie *Erastus* dyed:
Lord Marshall, hale them to the towers top,
And throw them headlong downe into the valley,
So let their treasons with their liues haue end.

    1. Witn. Your selfe procured vs. *2. Witn.* Is this our hier?
        Then the marshall beares them to the tower top.

  Soli. Speake not a word, least in my wrathfull furie,
I doome you to ten thousand direfull torments:
And *Brusor* see *Erastus* be interd,
VVith honor in a kingly sepulcher,
VVhy when Lord marshall? great *Hectors* sonne,
Although his age did plead for innocence :
VVas sooner tumbled from the fatall tower,
Then are those periurde wicked witnesses.

      Then they are both tumbled downe.

VVhy now *Erastus* Ghost is satisfied :
I, but yet the wicked Iudge suruiues,
By whome *Erastus* was condemnd to die,
Brusor, as thou louest me stab in the marshall,
Least he detect vs vnto the world,
By making knowne our bloudy practises,
And then will thou and I hoist saile to Rhodes,
VVhere thy *Lucina* and my *Perseda* liues.

  Bru. I wil my lord: lord Marshal, it is his highnes pleasure
That you commend him to *Erastus* soule.

      Then he kils the Marshall.

  Soli. Heere ends my deere *Erastus* tragedie,
And now begins my pleasant Comedie,
But if *Perseda* vnderstand these newes,
Our seane will prooue but tragicomicall.

  Bru. Feare not my Lord, *Lucina* plaies her part,
And wooes apace in *Solimans* behalfe.

  Soli. Then *Brusor* come, and with some few men,
Lets saile to Rhodes with all conuenient speede,
For till I sould *Perseda* in mine armes,
My troubled eares are deft with loues alarmes.   *Exeunt.*

    Enter Perseda, Lucina, *and* Basilisco.

        H 2   *Per.*

Perſe. Now ſignior *Baſiliſco,* which like you,
The Turkiſh or our nation beſt.

    Baſ. That which your ladiſhip will haue me like,

    Luci. I am deceiued but you were circumciſed,

    Baſ. Indeed I was a little cut in the porpuſe.

    Per. VVhat meanes made you to ſteale back to Rhodes,

    Baſ. The mightie pinckanied brand bearing God,
To whom I am ſo long true ſeruitour,
When he eſpyde my weeping flouds of teares,
For your depart, he bad me follow him:
I followed him, he with his fier brand,
Parted the ſeas, and we came ouer drieſhod.

    Luci. A matter not vnlikely : but how chance,
Your turkiſh bonet is not on your head ?

    Baſ. Becauſe I now am Chriſtian againe,
And that by naturall meanes, for as
The old Cannon ſaies verie pretily,
Nihill eſt tam naturali, quod eo modo colligatum eſt.
And ſo foorth : ſo *I* became a Turke to follow her,
To follow her, am now returnd a Chriſtian.

             Enter Piſton.

    Piſt. O Lady and miſtris, weepe and lament,
And wring your hands, for my Maiſter
Is condemnd and executed.

    Luci. Be patient ſweete *Perſeda,* the foole but ieſts,

    Perſe. Ah no, my nightly dreames foretould me this,
Which fooliſh woman fondly I neglected,
But ſay what death dyed my poore *Eraſtus* ?

    Piſt. Nay, God be praiſd, his death was reaſonable,
He was but ſtrangled,

    Perſe, But ſtrangled, ah double death to me,
But ſay, wherefore was he condemnd to die ?

    Piſt. For nothing but hie treaſon.

    Perſe. What treaſon, or by whom was he condemnd?

    Piſt. Faith two great knights of the poſt, ſwore vpon the
Alcaron, that he would haue firde the Turkes Fleete.

    Perſe. VVas *Bruſor* by ?

                                  Piſton

2100

2110

2120

2130

Piston. I.

Per. And *Soliman* ?

Pist. No but I saw where he stood,
To heere and see the matter well conuaid.

Perse. Accursed *Soliman,* prophane Alcaron,
Lucina, came thy husband to this end ?
To lead a Lambe vnto the slaughterhouse,
Hast thou for this, in *Solimans* behalfe ?
With cunning words tempted my chastitie,
Thou shalt abie for both your trecheries,
It must be so, *Basilisco* dooest thou loue me, speake,

Basi. I more then I loue either life or soule,
VVhat shall I stab the Emperout for thy sake.

Perse. No, but *Lucina* if thou louest me, kill her,
Then Basilisco *takes a Dagger & feeles vpon the point of it.*

Basi. The point will marre her skin.

Perse, What darest thou not, giue me the dagger then,
Theres a reward for all thy treasons past,

Then Perseda *kils* Lucina.

Basi. Yet dare I beare her hence, to do thee good ?

Perse. No let her lie, a pray to rauening birds:
Nor shall her death alone suffice for his,
Rhodes now shall be no longer *Solimans,*
VVeele fortifie our walles, and keepe the towne,
In spight of proud insulting *Soliman,*
I know the letcher hopes to haue my loue,
And first *Perseda,* shall with this hand die,
Then yeeld to him and liue in infamie.   *Exeunt.*

Manet Basilisco.

Basi. I will ruminate. Death which the poets
Faine to be pale and meager ;
Hath depriued Erastus trunke from breathing vitalitie,
A braue Cauelere, but my aprooued foeman:
Let me see: where is that Alcides, surnamed Hercules ?
The onely Club man of his time : dead.
VVhere is the eldest sonne of Pryam ?
That abraham couloured Troion : dead.

H 3   VVhere

VVhere is the leader of the Mirmidons,
That well knit *Accill*: dead.
VVhere is that furious *Aiax*, the sonne of *Telamon*,
Or that fraudfull squire of *Ithaca*, I clipt *Vlisses* ? dead,
VVhere is tipsie *Alexander*, that great cup conquerour,
Or *Pompey* that braue warriour ? dead:
I am my selfe strong, but I confesse death to be stronger,
I am valiant, but mortall,
I am adorned with natures gifs,
A giddie goddesse, that now giueth and anon taketh,
I am wise, but quiddits will not answer death :
To conclude in a word, to be captious, vertuous, ingenious,
Or to be nothing when it pleaseth death to be enuious.
The great Turque, whose seat is Constantinople,
Hath beleagred Rhodes, whose chieftaine is a woman.
I could take the rule vpon me,
But the shrub is safe when the Cedar shaketh:
I loue *Perseda* as one worthie,
But I loue *Basilisco* as one I hould more worthie.
My fathers sonne, my mothers solace, my proper selfe.
Faith he can doe little that cannot speake,
And he can doe lesse that cannot runne away.
Then sith mans life is as a glasse, and a phillip may cracke it,
Mine is no more and a bullet may pearce it:
Therefore I will play least in sight.   *Exit.*

 Enter Soliman, Brusor, with *Janisaries.*
 Soli. The gates are shut, which prooues that Rhodes re-
And that *Perseda* is not Solimans.   (uolts,
Ah *Brusor* see where thy *Lucina* lies
Butcherd dispightfullie without the walles.
 Bru. Vnkinde *Perseda*, couldst thou vse her so?
And yet we vs'd *Perseda* little better.
 Soli. Nay gentle *Brusor* stay thy teares a while,
Least with thy woes thou spoile my commedie,
And all to soone be turnd to Tragedies.
Go *Brusor*, beare her to thy priuate tent,
Where we at leasure will lament her death,

                                        And

62

And with our teares bewaile her obsequies:
For yet *Perseda* liues for *Soliman.*
Drum sound a parle, were it not for her,
I would sacke the towne ere I would sound a parle.
      The Drum soundes a parle.
  Perseda comes vpon the walles in mans apparell
   Basilisco and Piston *vpon the walles.*
 Per. At whose intreatie is this parle sounded?
 Soli. At our intreaty, therefore yeeld the towne.
 Per. Why what art thou that boldly bids vs yeeld?
 Soli. Great *Soliman,* Lord of all the world.
 Per. Thou art not Lord of all, Rhodes is not thine.
 Soli. It was, and shall be maugre who saies no.
 Per. I that say no will neuer see it thine.
 Soli. Why what art thou that dares resist my force?
 Per. A Gentleman and thy mortall enemie,
And one that dares thee to the single combate:
 Soli. First tell me, dooth *Perseda* liue or no?
  Per. She liues to see the wrack of *Soliman,*
 Soli. Then ile combate thee what ere thou art.
 Per. And in *Erastus* name ile combat thee,
And heere I promise thee on my Christian faith,
Then will I yeeld *Perseda* to thy hands,
That if thy strength shall ouermatch my right,
To vse, as to thy liking shall seeme best,
But ere I come to enter single fight,
First let my tongue vtter my hearts despight,
And thus my tale begins : thou wicked tirant,
Thou murtherer, accursed homicide,
For whome hell gapes, and all the vgly feends
Do waite for to receiue thee in their iawes:
Ah periur'd and inhumaine Soliman,
How could thy heart harbour a wicked thought?
Against the spotlesse life of poore *Erastus*?
VVas he not true? would thou hadst been as iust,
VVas he not valiant? would thou hadst bin as vertuous,
VVas he not loyall? would thou hadst been as louing:
            Ah

Ah wicked tirant in that one mans death,
Thou haft betrayde the flower of Chriftendome,
Dyed he becaufe his worth obfcured thine,
In flaughtering him thy vertues are defamed,
Didft thou mifdoe him, in hope to win *Perfeda,*
Ah foolifh man, therein thou art deceiued,
For though fhe liue, yet will fhe neare liue thine,
VVhich to approoue, ile come to combat thee.

*Soli.*Iniurious foule mouthd knight, my wrathfull arme
Shall chaftife and rebuke thefe iniuries.

         T hen Perfeda *comes downe to* Soliman, *and*
              Bafilifco *and* Pifton.

Pift. I but heere you, are you fo foolifh to fight with him?
Baf. I firra, why not, as long as I ftand by?
Soli. Ile not defend *Eraftus* innocence,
But thee, maintianing of *Perfedas* beautie,

        Then they fight, Solim an *kils* Perfeda.

Per. I now *I* lay *Perfeda* at thy feete,
But with thy hand firft wounded to the death,
Now fhall the world report that *Soliman,*
Slew *Eraftus* in hope to win *Perfeda,*
And murtherd her for louing of hir husband.

Soli. What my *Perfeda,*ah what haue I doone,
Yet kiffe me gentle loue before thou die.

Perfe. A kiffe I graunt thee, though I hate thee deadly.

Soli. I loued thee deerelie and accept thy kiffe,
VVhy didft thou loue *Eraftus* more then me,
Or why didft not giue *Soliman* a kiffe
Ere this vnhappie time, then hadft thou liued?

*Bafi.*Ah let me kiffe thee too before *I* die,

          Then Soliman *kils* Bafilifco.

*Soli.*Nay die thou fhalt for thy prefumption,
For kiffing her whom *I* do hould fo deare,

Pift. I will not kiffe hir fir, but giue me leaue
To weepe ouer hir, for while fhe liued,
Shee loued me deerely, and *I* loued hir.

*Soli.*If thou didft loue hir villaine as thou faidft,

                   Then

2250

2260

2270

2280

Then wait on her thorough eternall night.

Then Soliman *kils* Piston.

Ah *Perseda*, how shall I mourne for thee?
Faire springing rose, ill pluckt before thy time.
Ah heauens that hitherto haue smilde on me,
Why doe you vnkindly lowre on *Soliman*?
The losse of halfe my Realmes, nay crownes decay,
Could not haue prickt so neere vnto my heart,
As doth the losse of my *Persedaes* life:
And with her life, I likewise loose my loue,
And with her loue my hearts felicitie,
Euen for *Erastus* death, the heauens haue plagued me.
Ah no the heauens did neuer more accurse me,
Then when they made me Butcher of my loue,
Yet iustly how can I condemne my selfe,
When *Brusor* liues that was the cause of all.
Come *Brusor*, helpe to lift her bodie vp,
Is she not faire?
   Bru. Euen in the houre of death.
   Soli. Was she not constant?
   Bru. As firme as are the poles whereon heauen lies.
   Soli. VVas she not chaste?
   Bru. As is *Pandora* or *Dianaes* thoughts.
   Soli. Then tell me? his treasons set aside,
VVhat was *Erastus* in thy opinion?
   Bru. Faire spoken, wise, curteous, and liberall:
Kinde, euen to his foes, gentle and affable,
And all, in all, his deeds heroyacall.
   Soli. Ah, was he so? how durst thou then vngratious
First cause me murther such a worthy man,   (Counseller,
And after tempt so vertuous a woman,
Be this therefore the last that ere thou speake:
Ianisaries, take him straight vnto the block,
Off with his head, and suffer him not to speake.

      Exit Brusor.

And now *Perseda* heere I lay me downe,
And on thy beautie still contemplate,

        I   Vntill

Vntill mine eyes shall surfet by my gasing:
But stay let me see what paper is this.

Then be takes vp a paper, and reades in it as followeth.

Tyrant my lips were sawst with deadly poyson,
To plague thy hart that is so full of poison.

What am I poisoned? then Ianisaries,
Let me see Rhodes recouerd ere I die,
Souldiers, assault the towne on euery side,
Spoile all, kill all, let none escape your furie,
            Sound an alarum to the fight.
Say Captaine, is Rhodes recouered againe.
    Capt. It is my Lord, and stoopes to *Soliman.*
    Soli. Yet that alayes the furie of my paine,
Before I die, for doubtlesse die I must,
I fates, iniurious fates, haue so decreed,
For now I feele the poyson gins to worke,
And I am weake euen to the very death,
Yet some thing more contentedly I die,
For that my death was wrought by her deuise,
Who liuing was my ioy, whose death my woe.
Ah Ianisaries now dyes your Emperour,
Before his age hath seene his mellowed yeares,
And if you euer loued your Emperour,
Affright me not with sorrowes and laments,
And when my soule from body shall depart,
Trouble me not but let me passe in peace,
And in your silence let your loue be showne:
My last request for I commaund no more,
Is that my body, with *Persedas* be,
Interd, where my *Erastus* lyes intombd,
And let one Epitaph containe vs all:
Ah now I feele the paper tould me true,
The poison is disperst through euery vaine,
And boiles like Etna in my frying guts,
Forgiue me deere *Erastus* my vnkindnes:

I

I haue reuengd thy deaths with many deaths,
And sweete *Perseda* flie not *Soliman,*
When as my gliding ghost shall follow thee,
With eager moode, thorow eternall night:
And now pale Death sits on my panting soule,
And with reuenging ire dooth tyrannise:
And saies for *Solimans* too much amisse,
This day shall be the peryod of my blisse.   *Exeunt.*
　　　Then Soliman dyes, and they carry him forth with silence.

　　　　　　Enter Chorus.
　Fortune. I gaue *Erastus* woe and miserie,
Amidst his greatest ioy and iollitie.
　Loue. But I that haue power in earth and heauen aboue,
Stung them both with neuer failing loue.
　Death. But I bereft them both of loue and life.
　Loue. Of life, but not of loue, for euen in death,
Their soules are knit, though bodies be disioynd,
Thou didst but wound their flesh, their minds are free,
Their bodies buried, yet they honour me.
　Death. Hence foolish *Fortune,* and thou wanton *Loue,*
Your deedes are trifles, mine of consequence,
　Fortune. I giue worlds happines, and woes increase.
　Loue. By ioyning persons, I increase the world.
　Death. By wasting all, I conquer all the world,
And now to end our difference at last,
In this last act, note but the deedes of death,
VVhere is *Erastus* now but in my triumph?
VVhere are the murtherers but in my triumph?
VVheres iudge and witnesse but in my triumph?
Wheres falce *Lucina* but in my triumph?
Wheres faire *Perseda* but in my triumph?
VVheres *Basilisco* but in my triumph?
VVheres faithfull *Piston* but in my triumph?
VVheres valiant *Brusor* but in my triumph?
And wheres great *Soliman* but in my triumph?
Their loues and fortunes ended with their liues,
　　　　　　　　I 2　　　　　　　. And

67

And they muſt wait vpon the Carre of death:
Packe *Loue* and *Fortune*, play in Commedies,
For powerfull death beſt ſitteth Tragedies.

Loue. I go, yet *Loue* ſhall neuer yeeld to *Death*.

Exit Loue.

Death. But *Fortune* ſhall, for when I waſte the world,
Then times and kingdomes *Fortunes* ſhall decay.

For. Meane time will *Fortune* gouerne as ſhe may.

Exit Fortune.

Death. I now will *Death* in his moſt haughtie pride,
Fetch his imperiall Carre from deepeſt hell,
And ride in triumph through the wicked world,
Sparing none but ſacred *Cynthias* friend,
Whome *Death* did feare before her life began,
For holy fates haue grauen it in their tables,
That *Death* ſhall die if he attempt her end,
VVhoſe life is heauens delight and *Cynthias* friend.

FINIS.

Imprinted at London for *Edward*
White, and are to be ſold at his ſhop, at the
little North doore of S. Paules Church
at the ſigne of the Gunne.